Fucking Relax

An adult coloring book of spiritual wisdom and hand-drawn mandala designs

©2016 LifeMath Publishing

ISBN 978-0-9863098-3-0

Author + Illustrator: Alexandra Love Sarton

www.alexandra.love

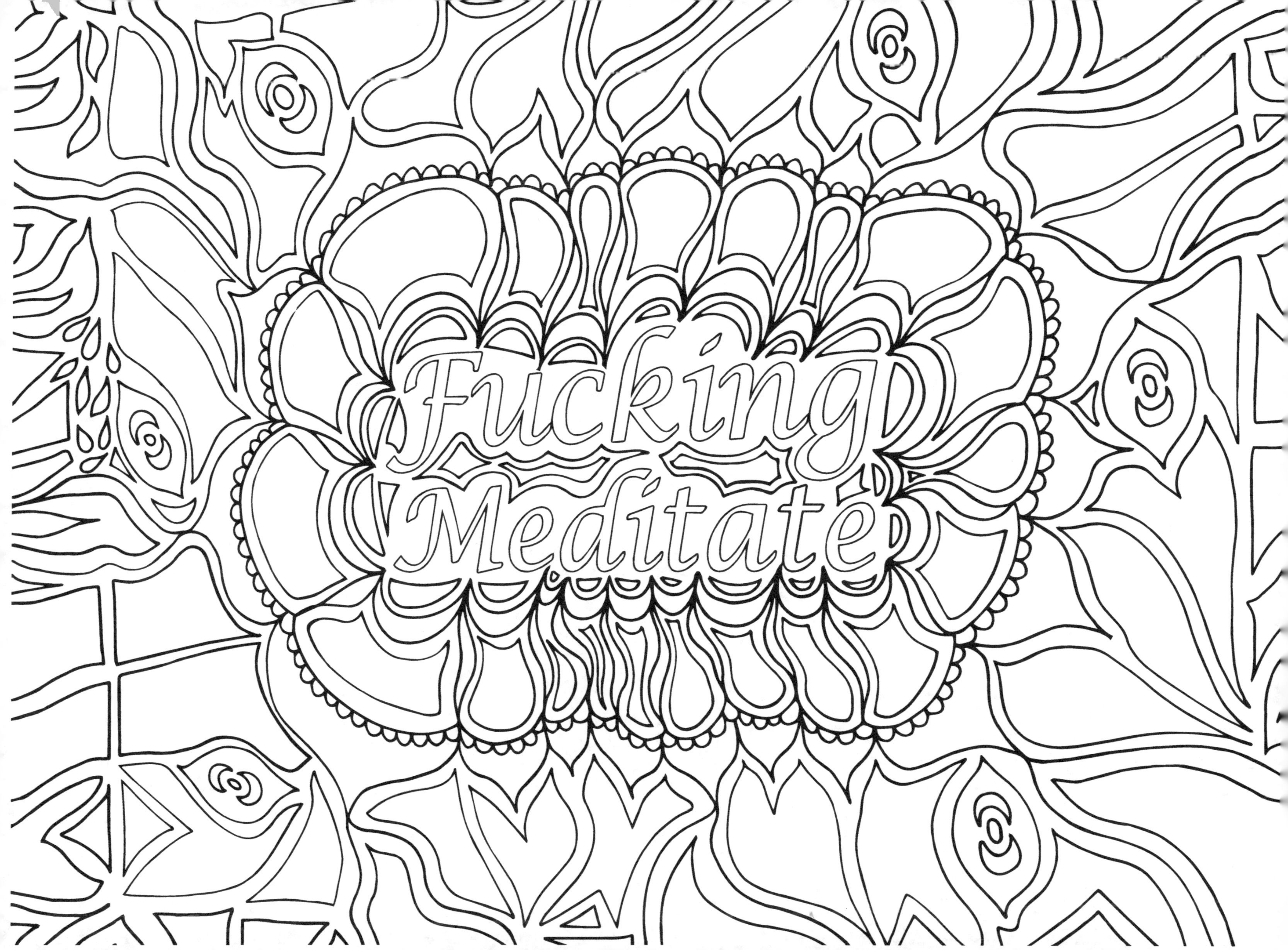
Fucking
Meditate

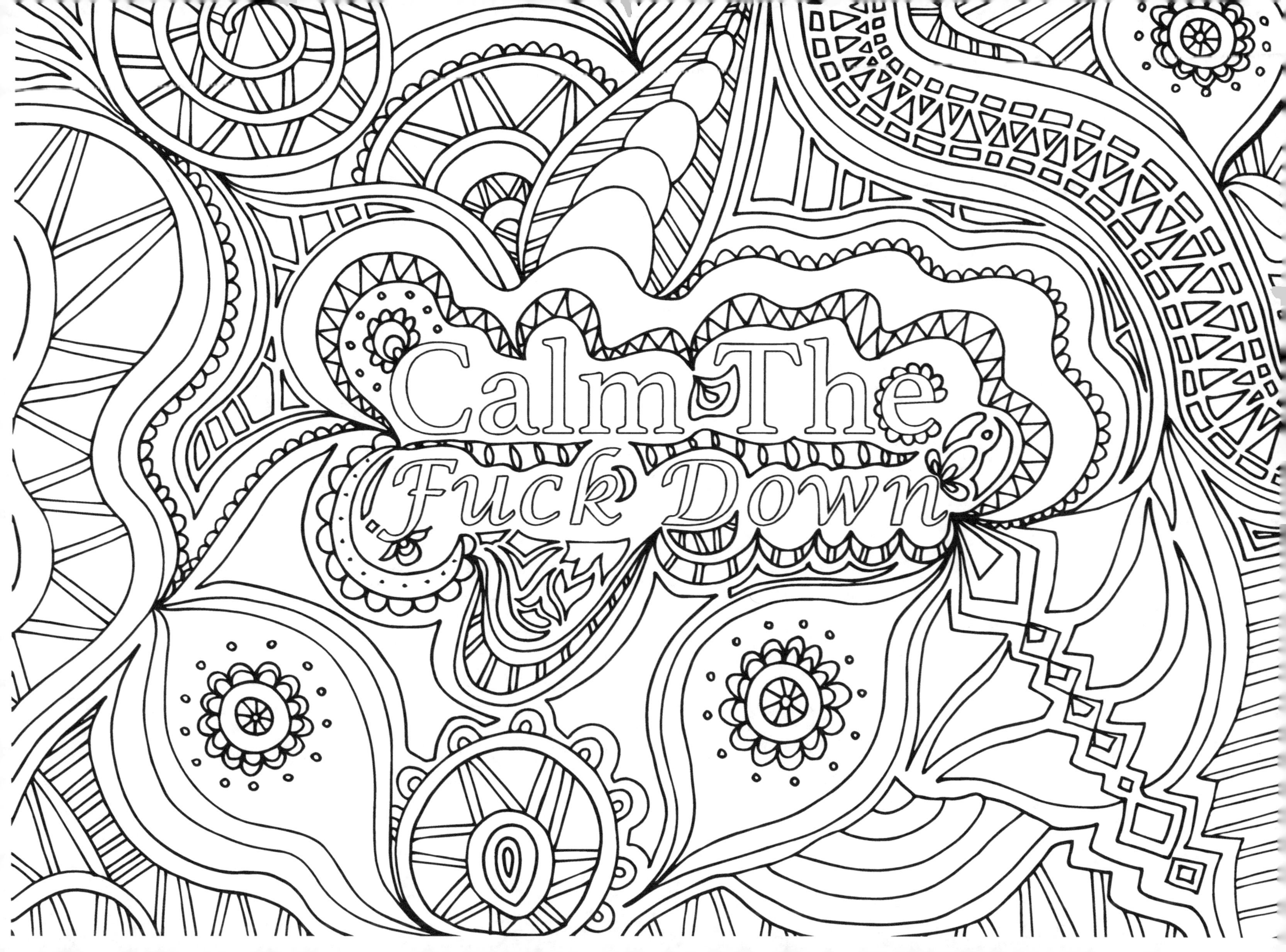

Calm The
Fuck Down

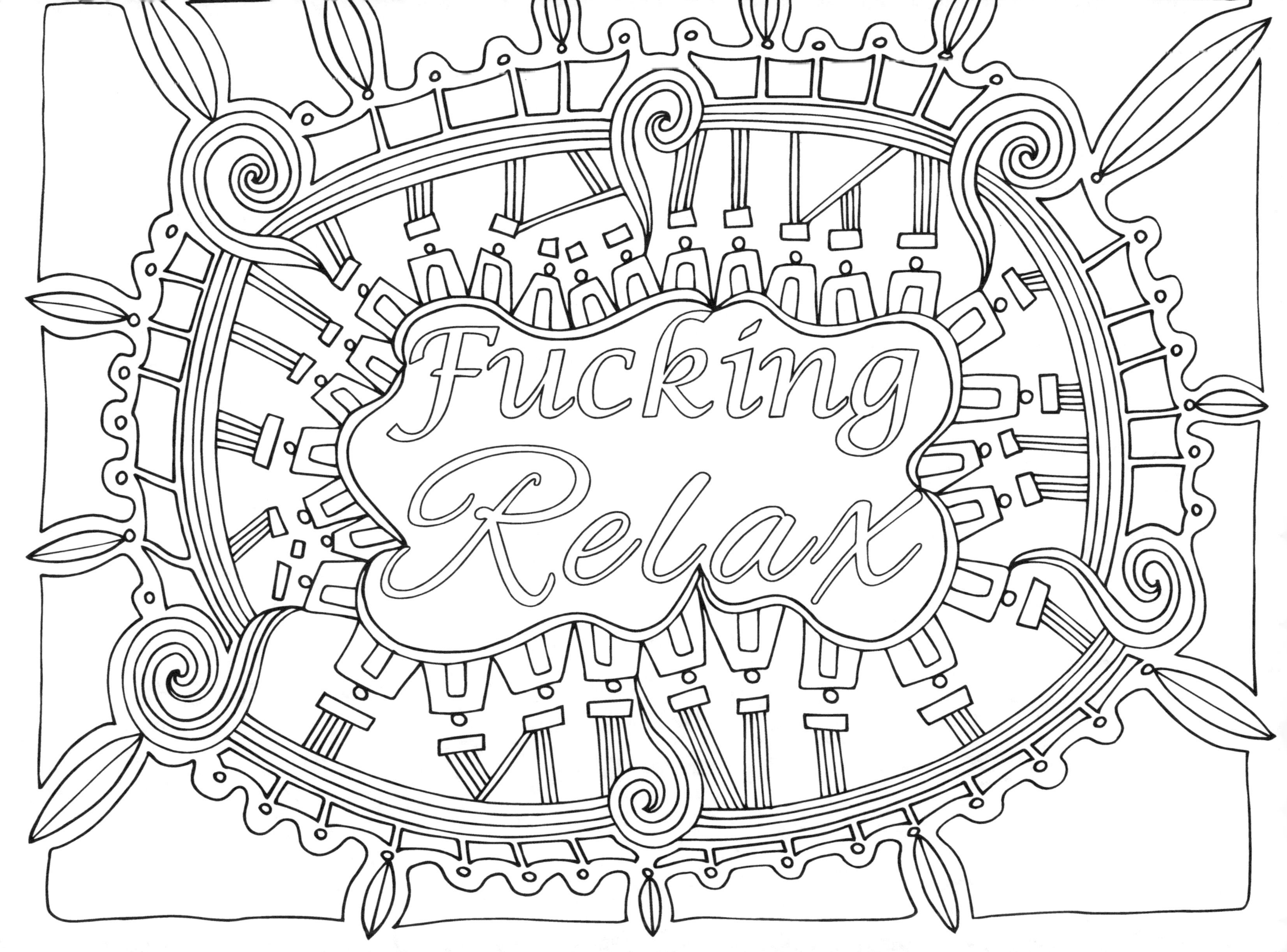
Fucking
Relax

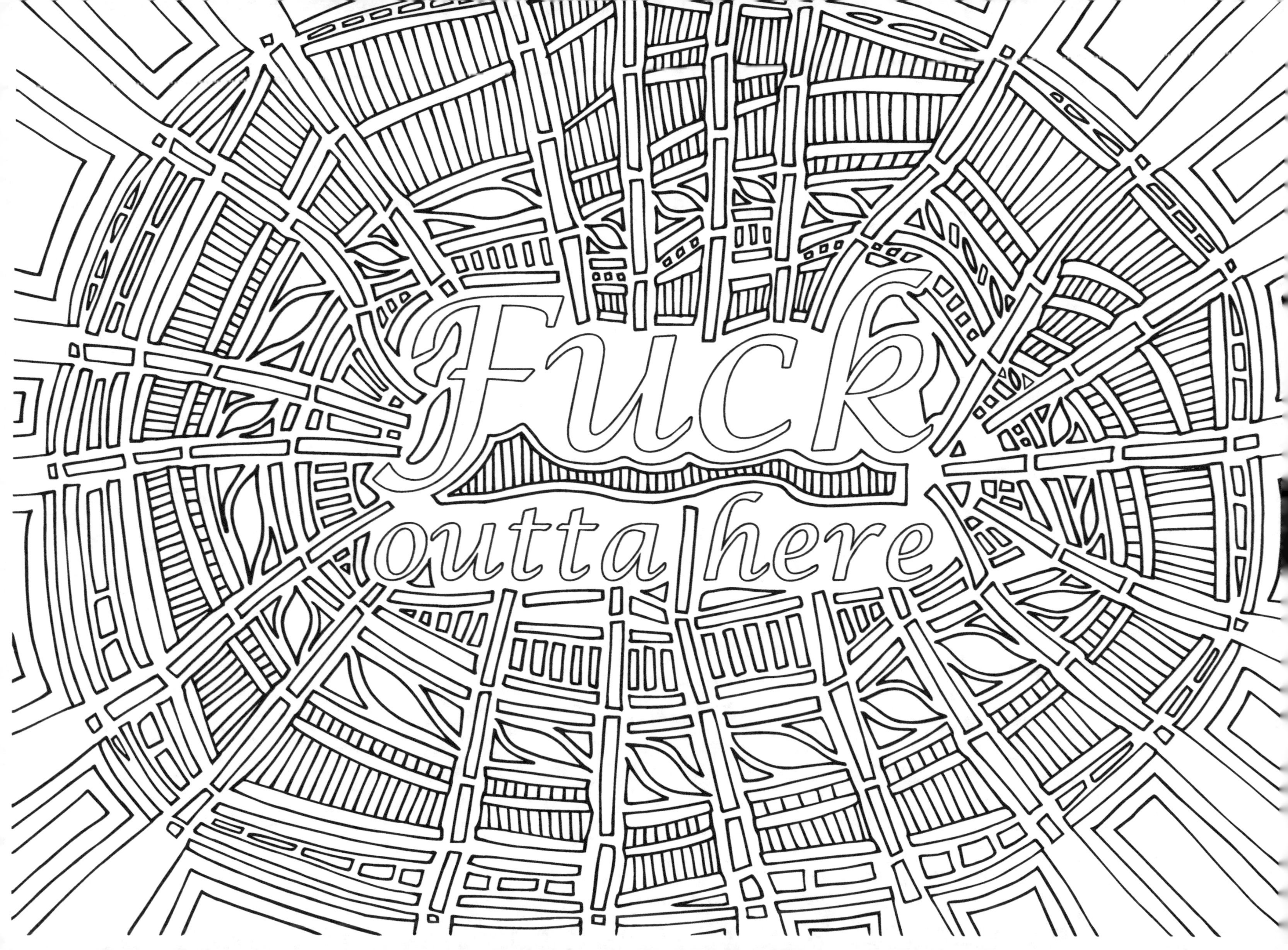

Fuck
outta here

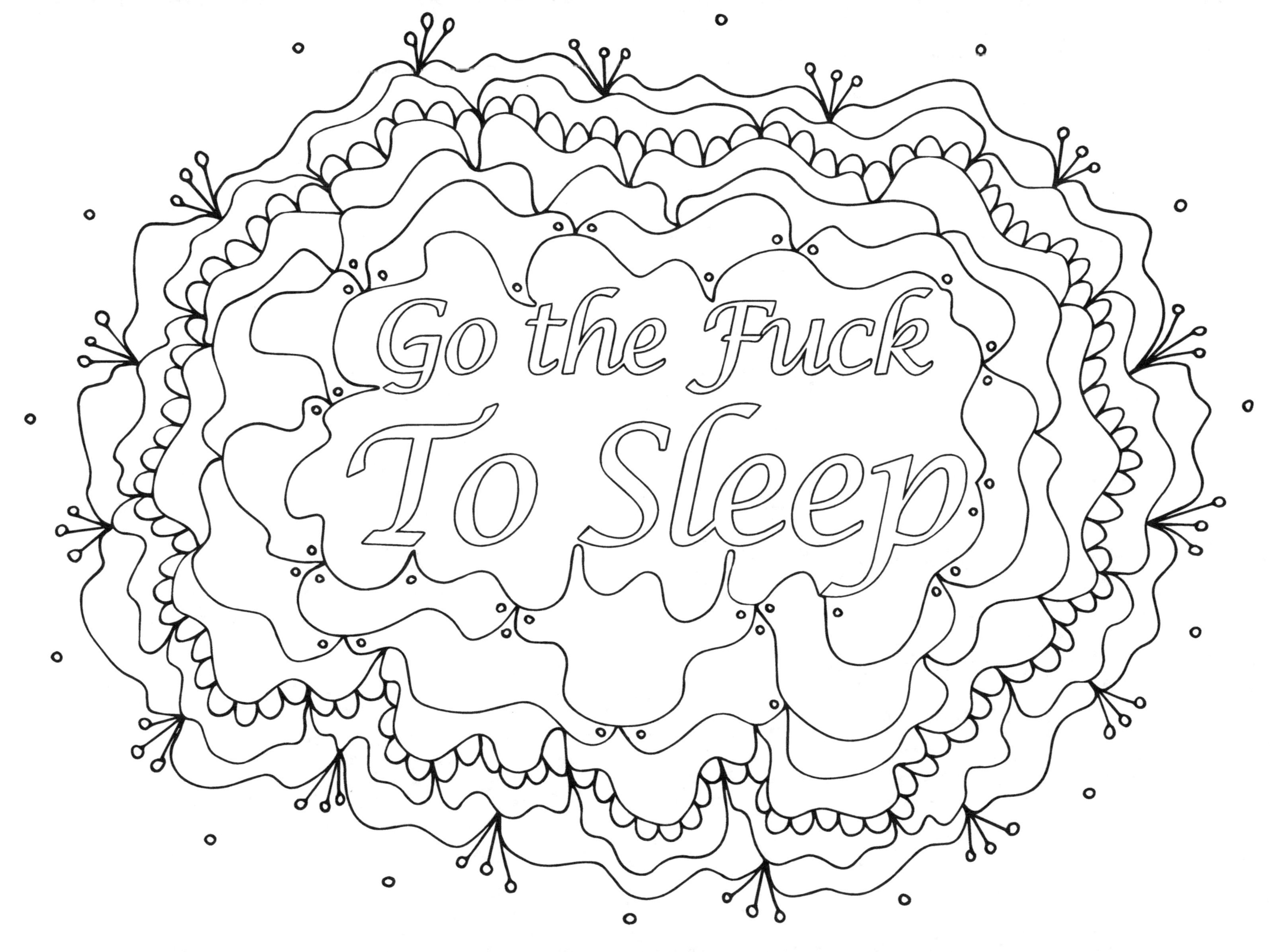
Go the Fuck
To Sleep

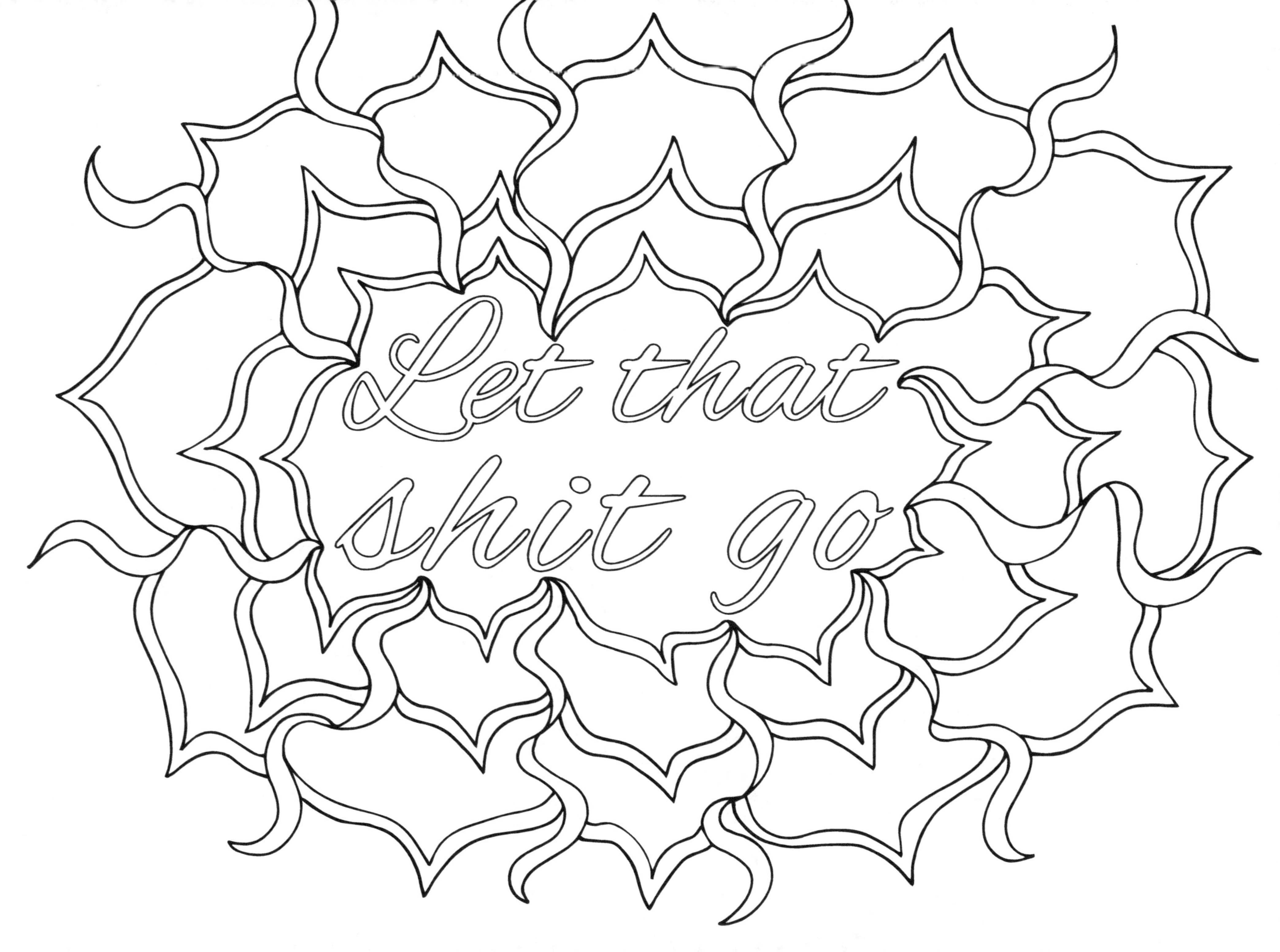

Let that
shit go

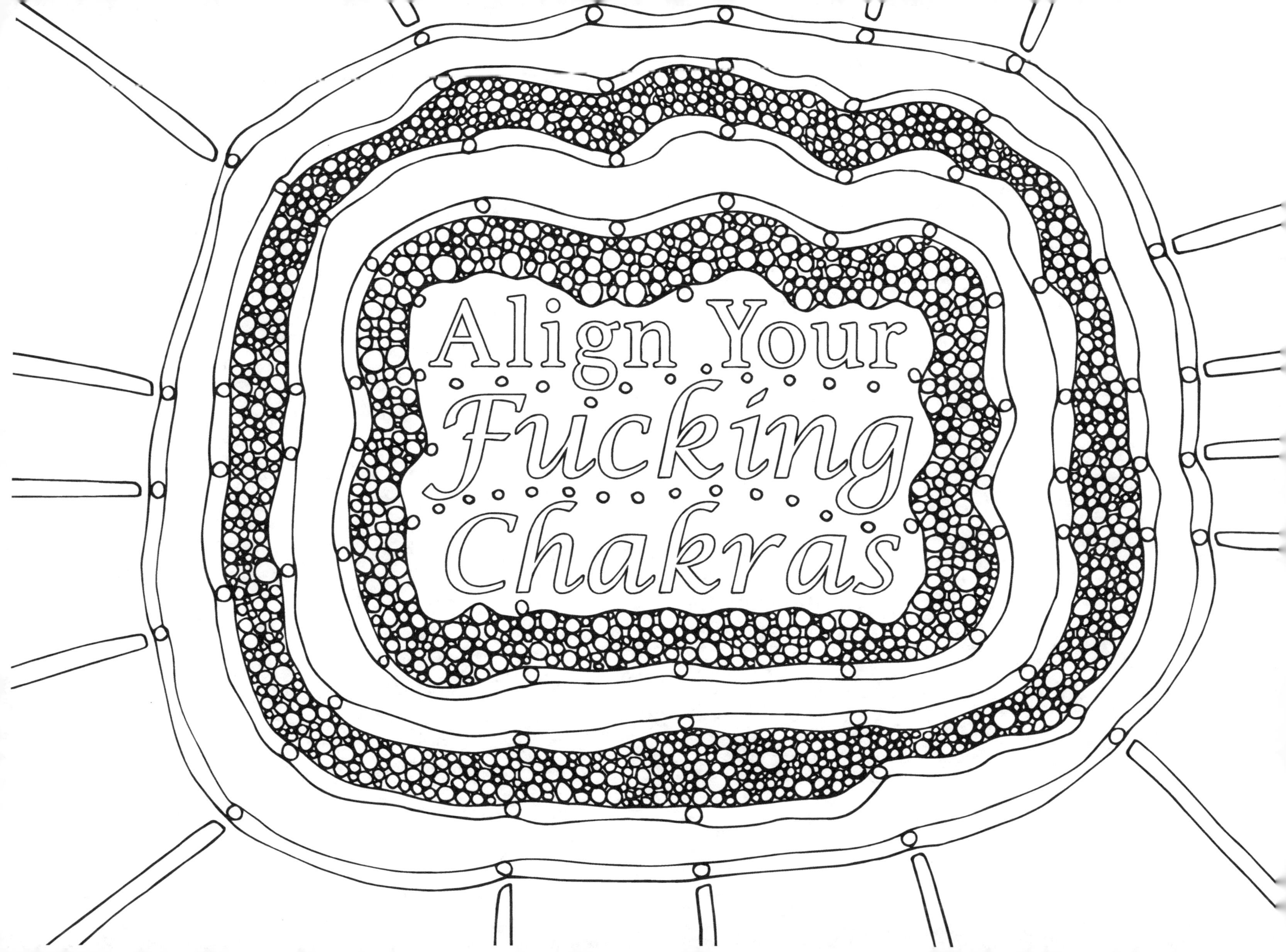

Align Your
Fucking
Chakras

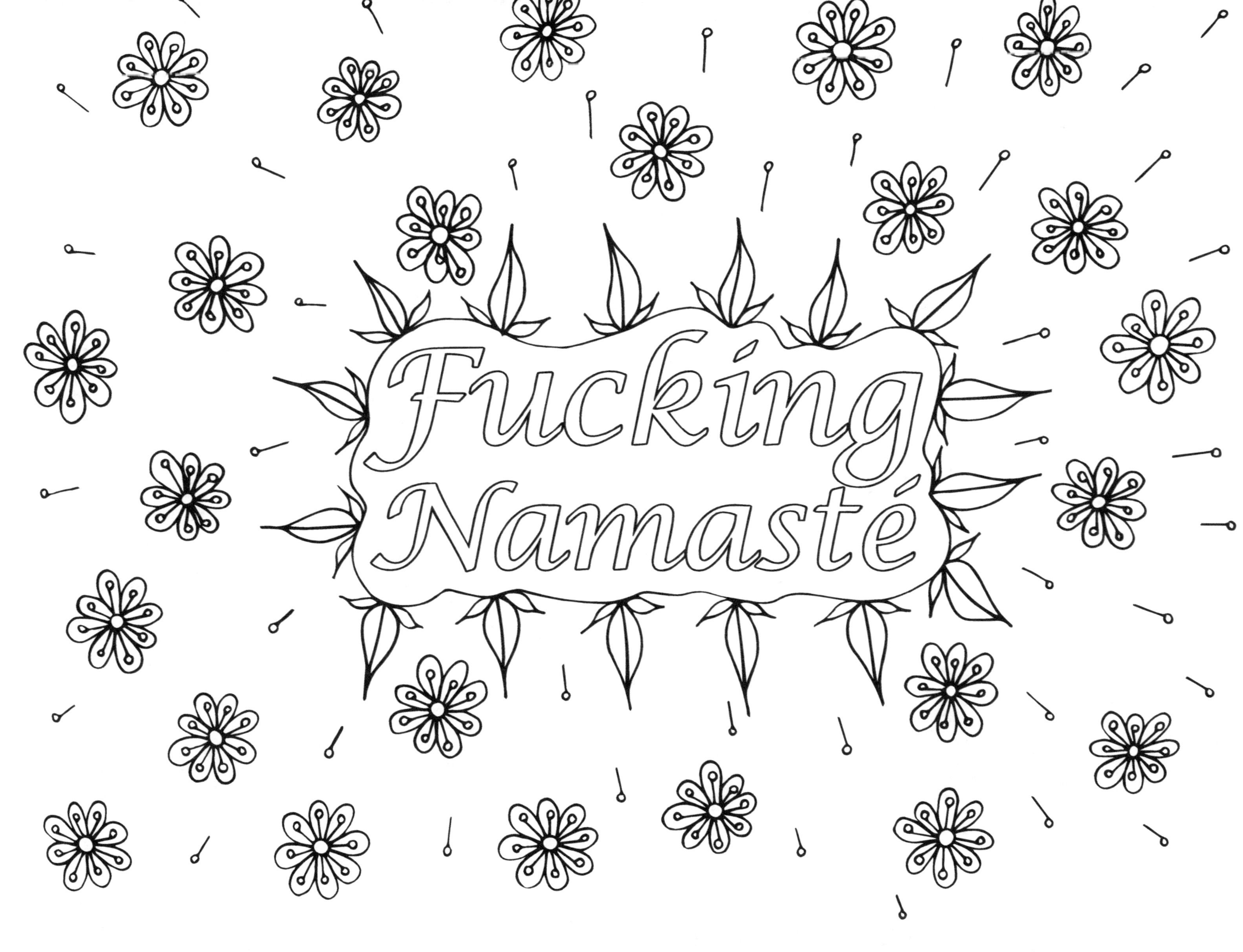
Fucking Namasté

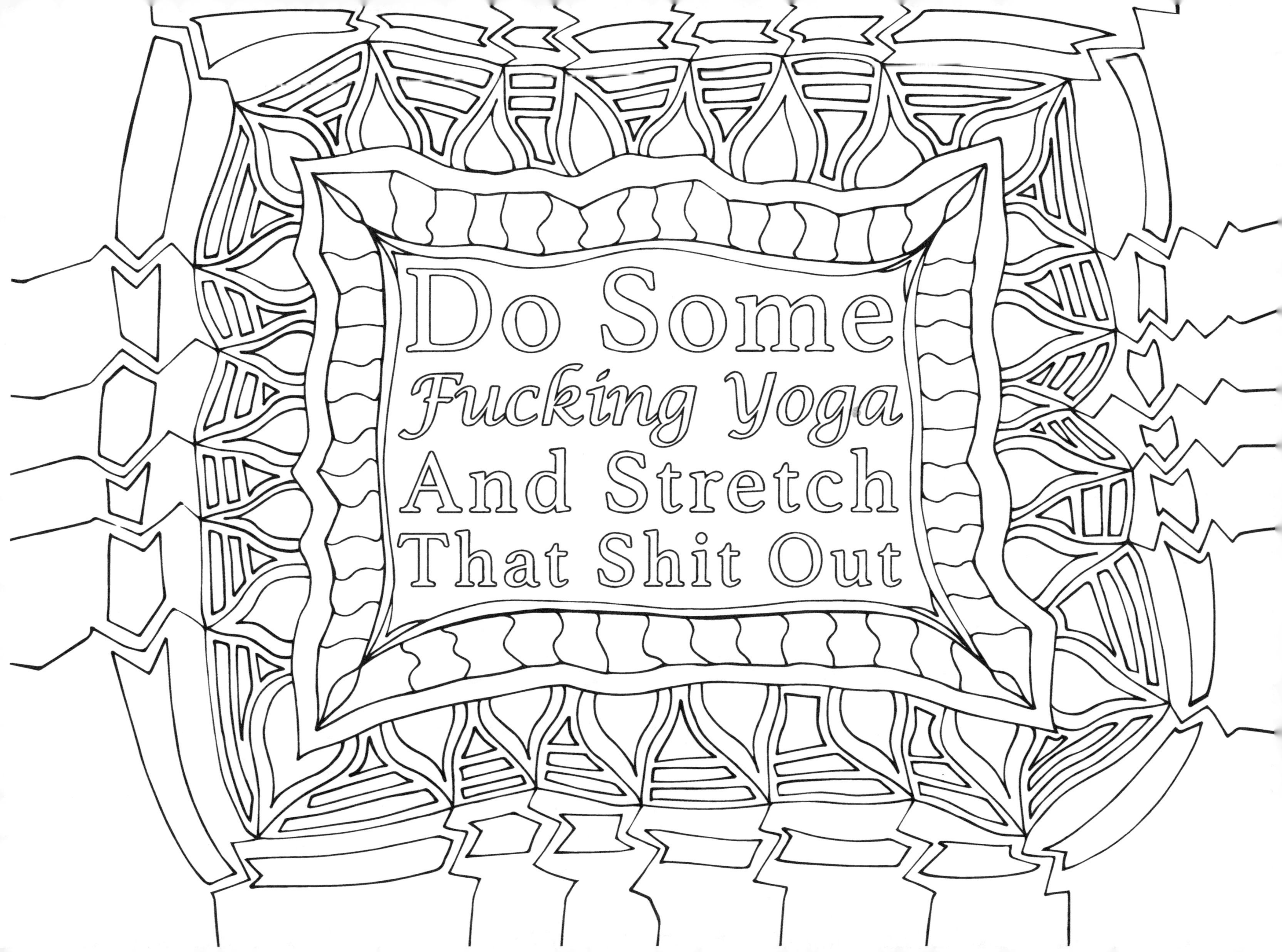

Do Some
Fucking Yoga
And Stretch
That Shit Out

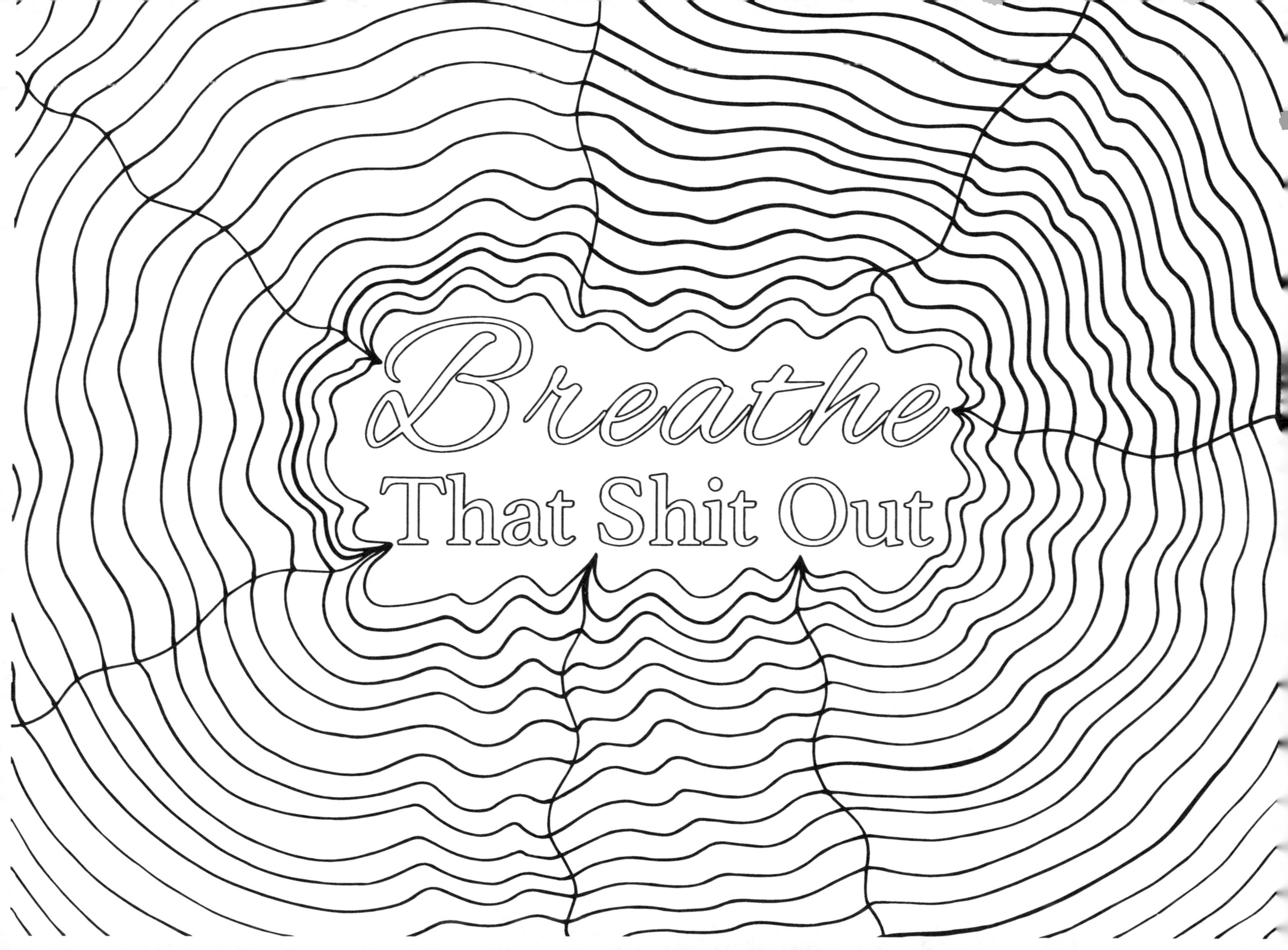
Breathe
That Shit Out

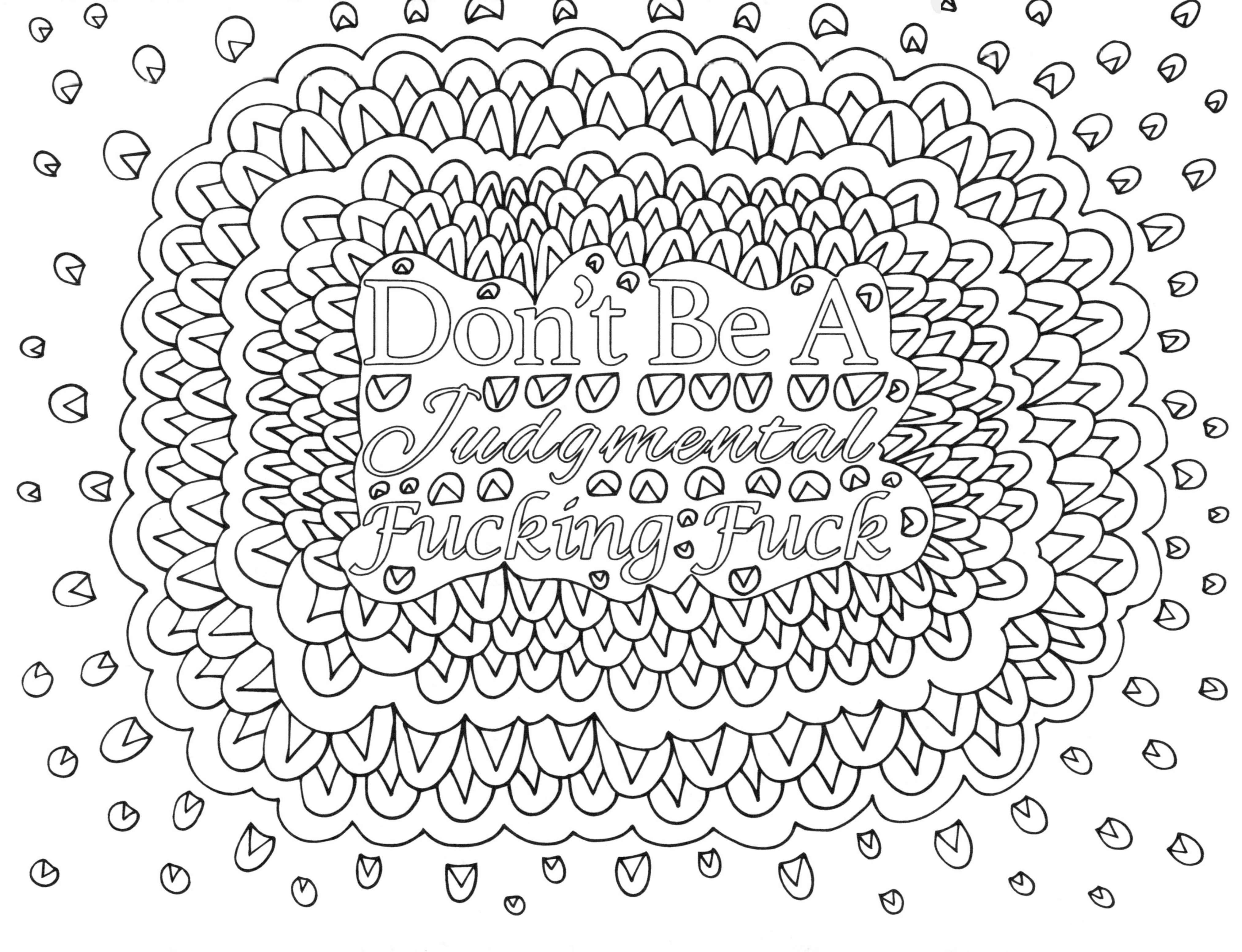

Don't Be A
Judgmental
Fucking Fuck

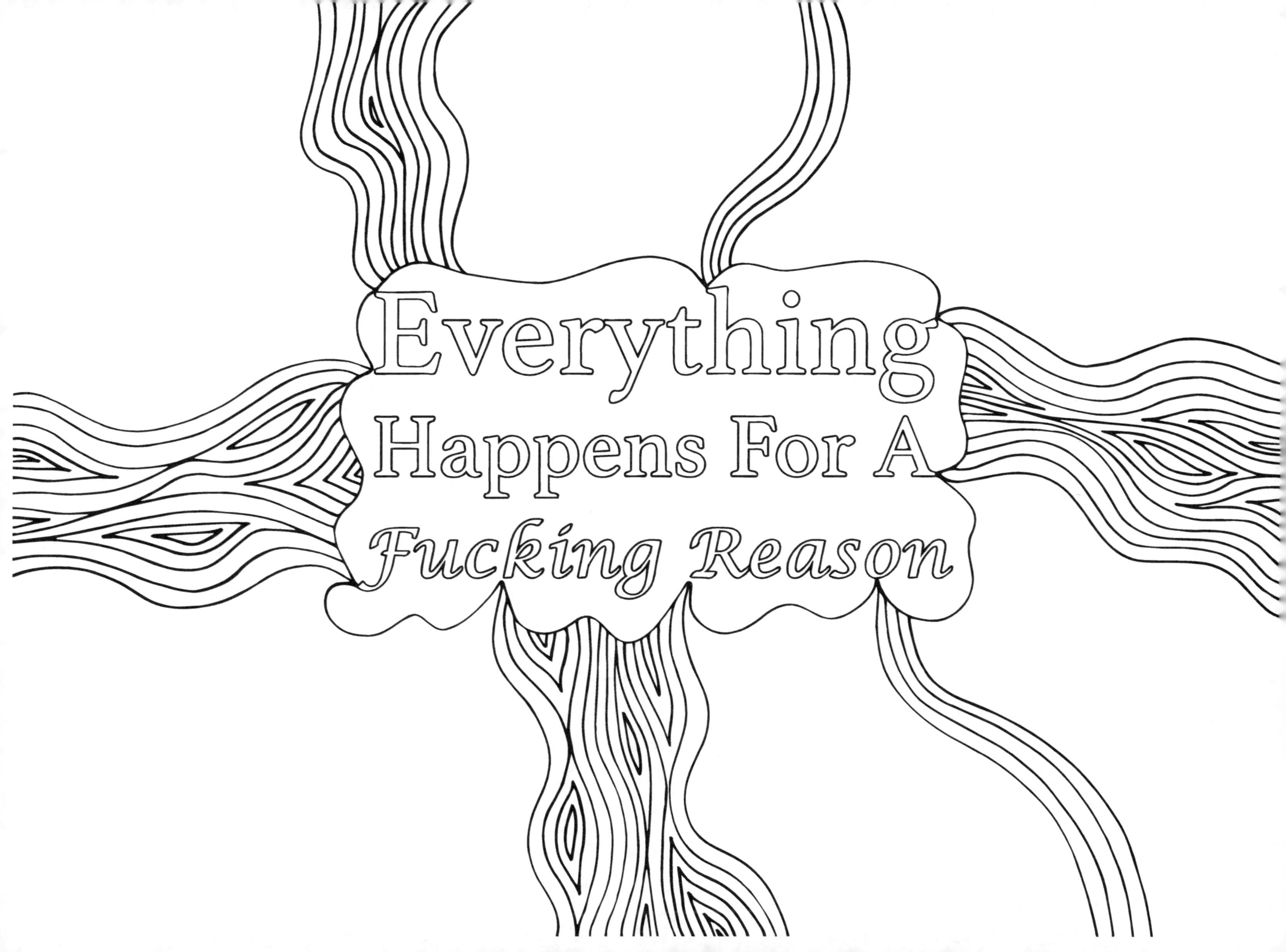

Everything
Happens For A
Fucking Reason

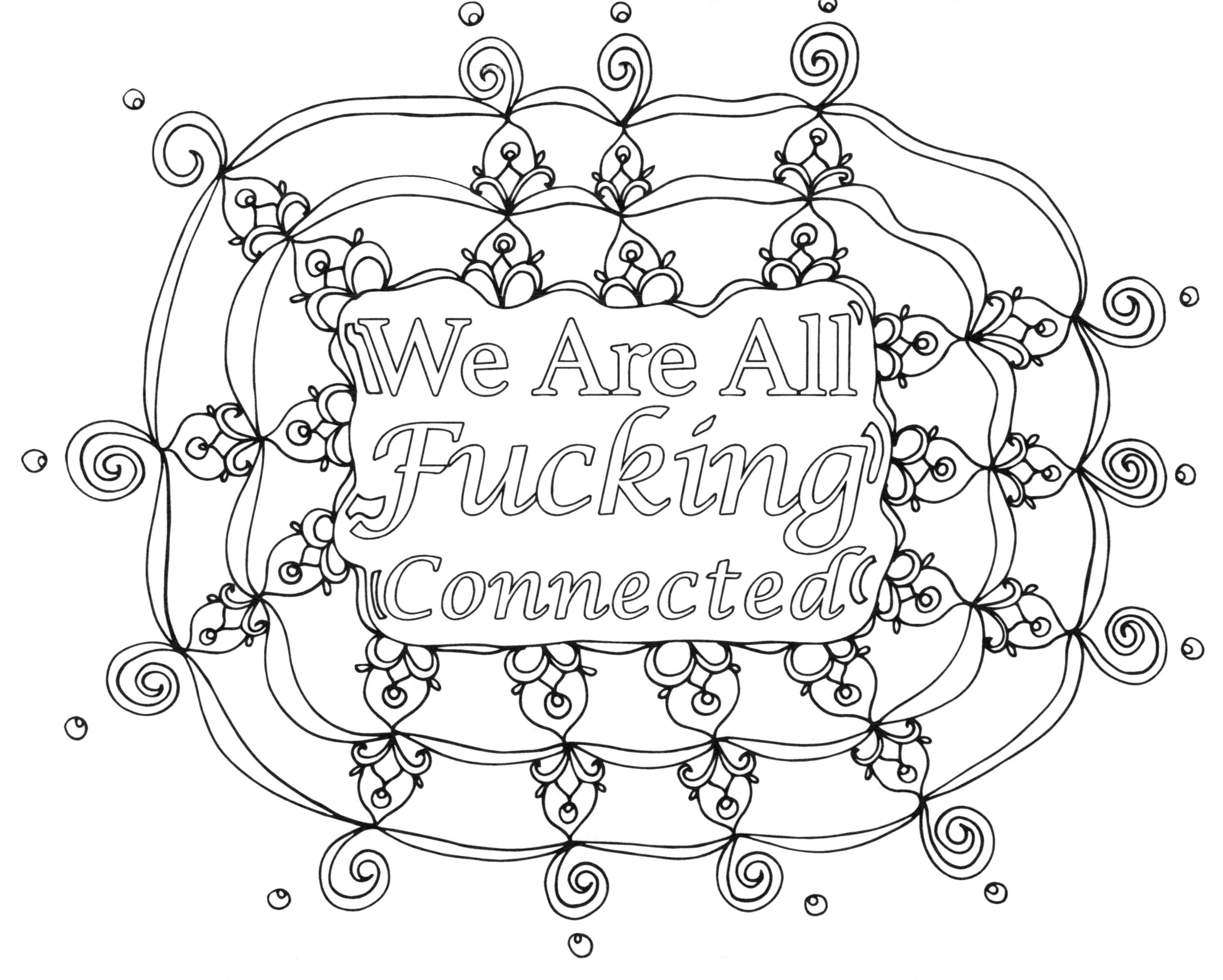

We Are All
Fucking
Connected

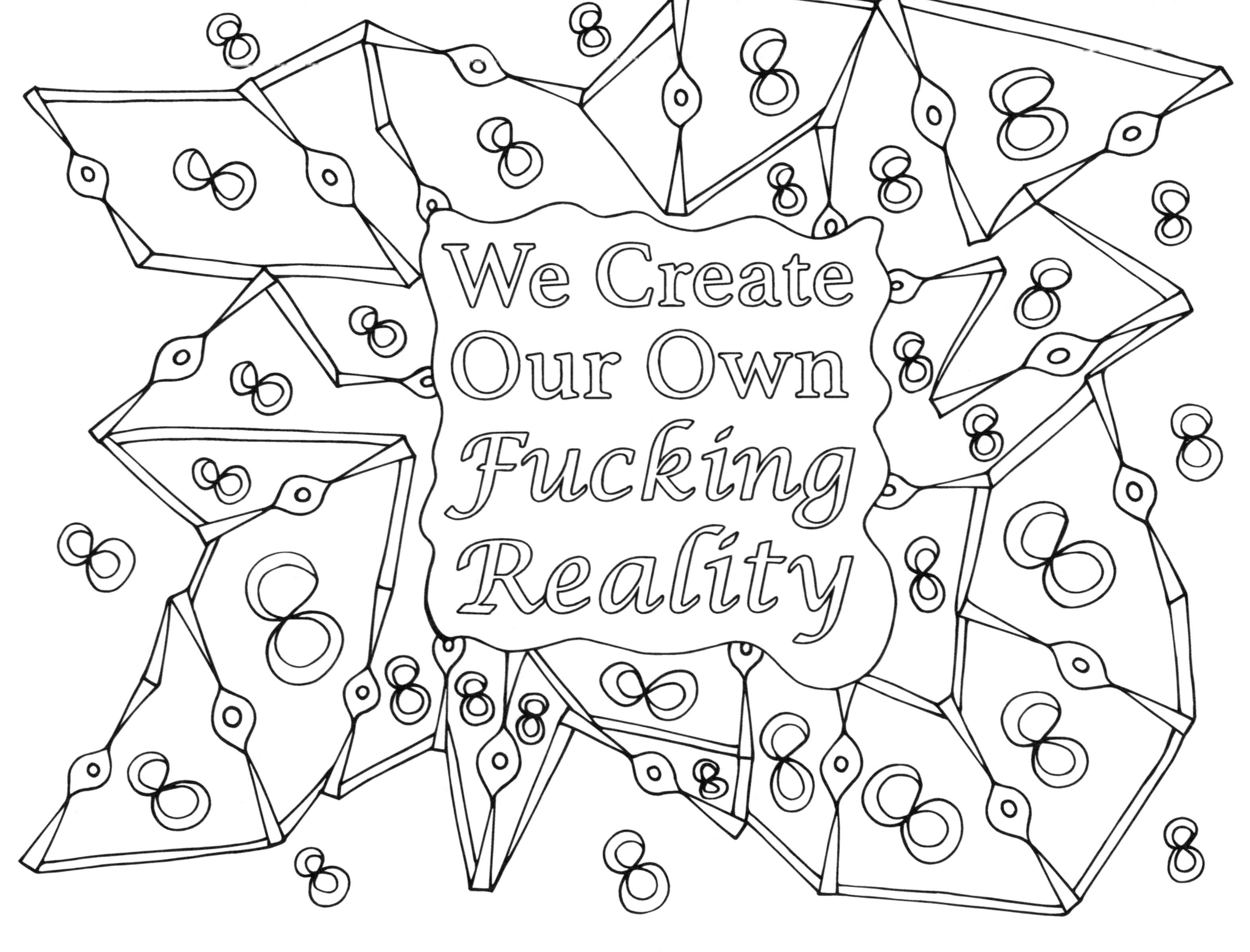

We Create
Our Own
Fucking
Reality

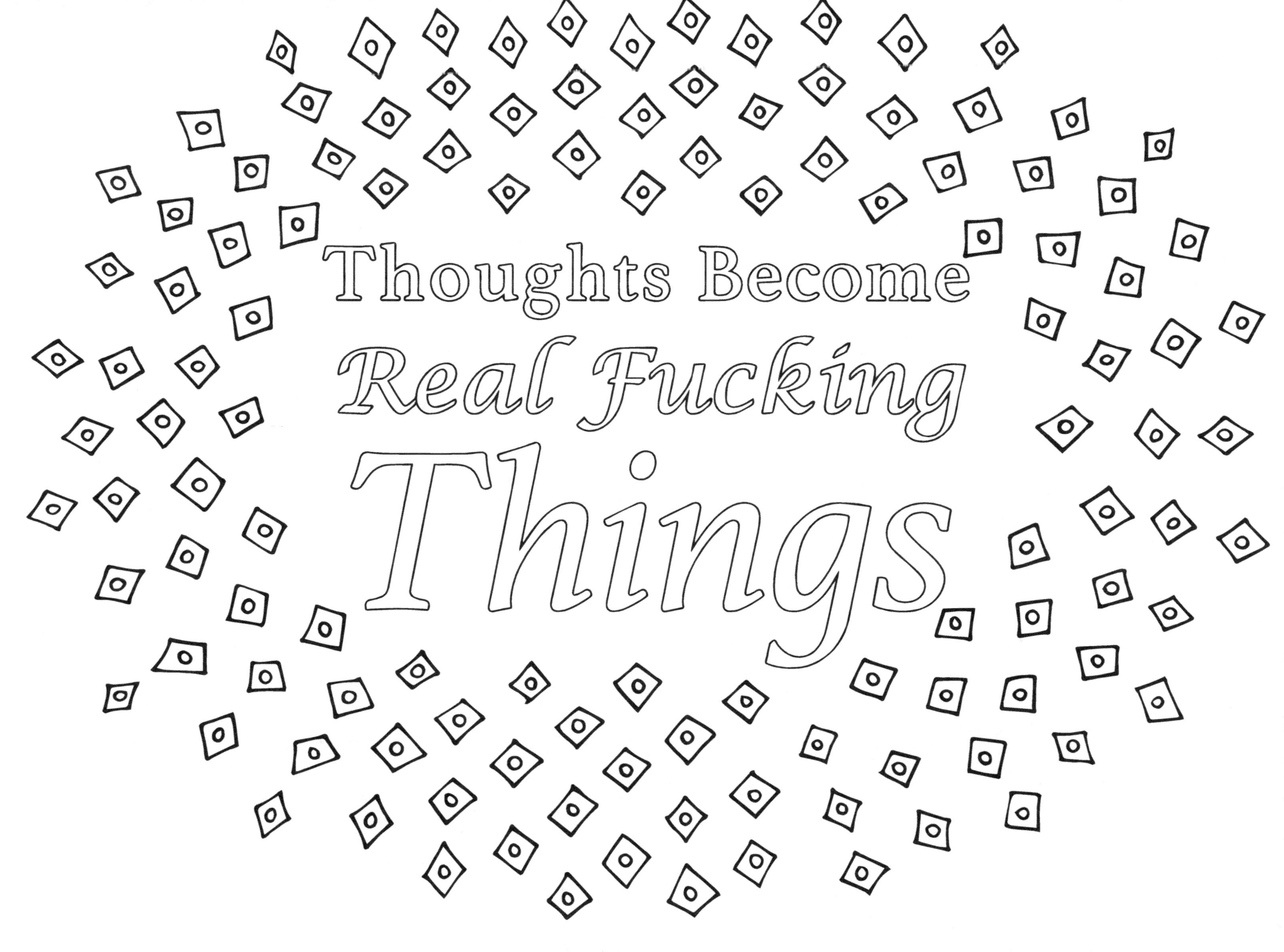

Thoughts Become
Real Fucking
Things

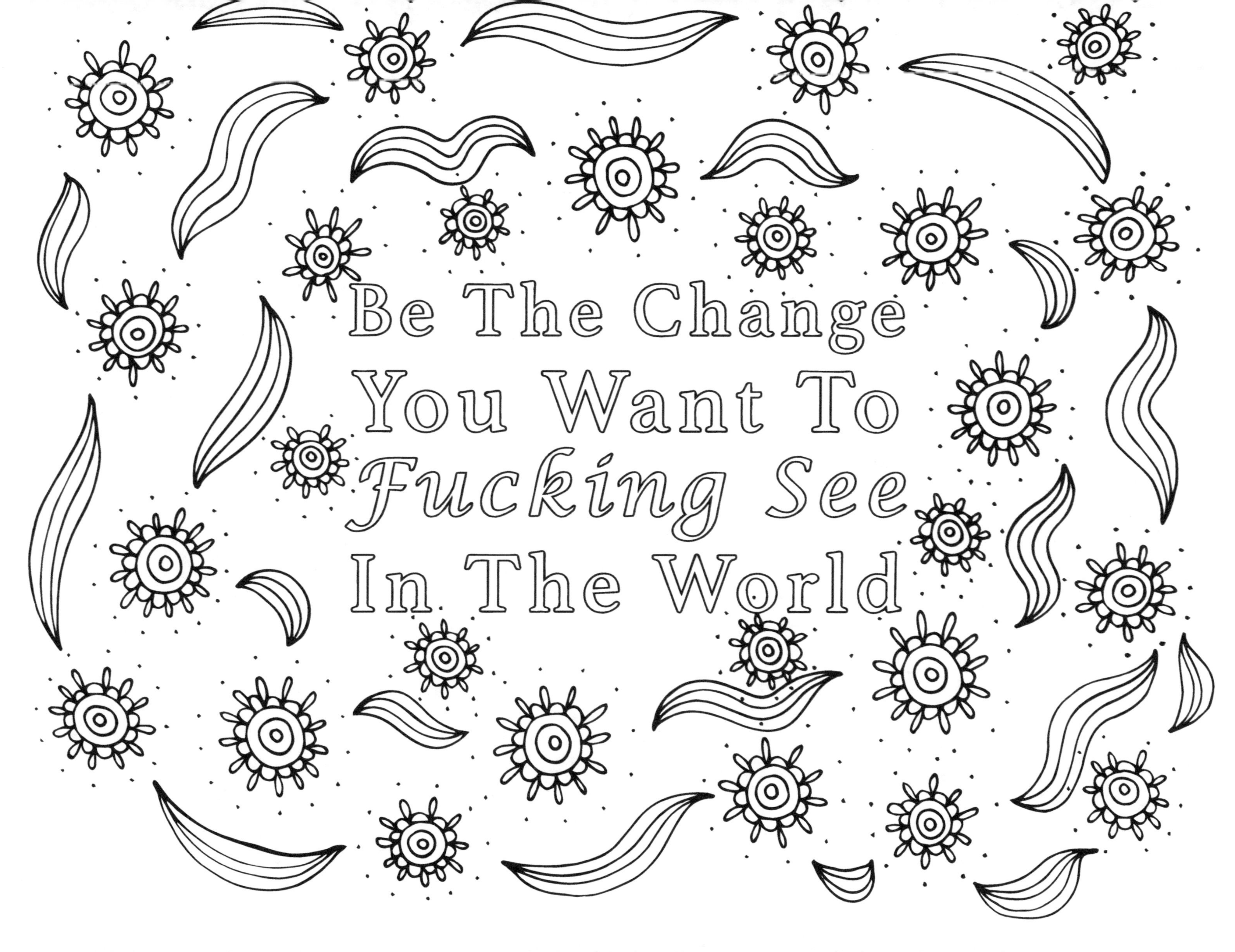

Be The Change
You Want To
Fucking See
In The World

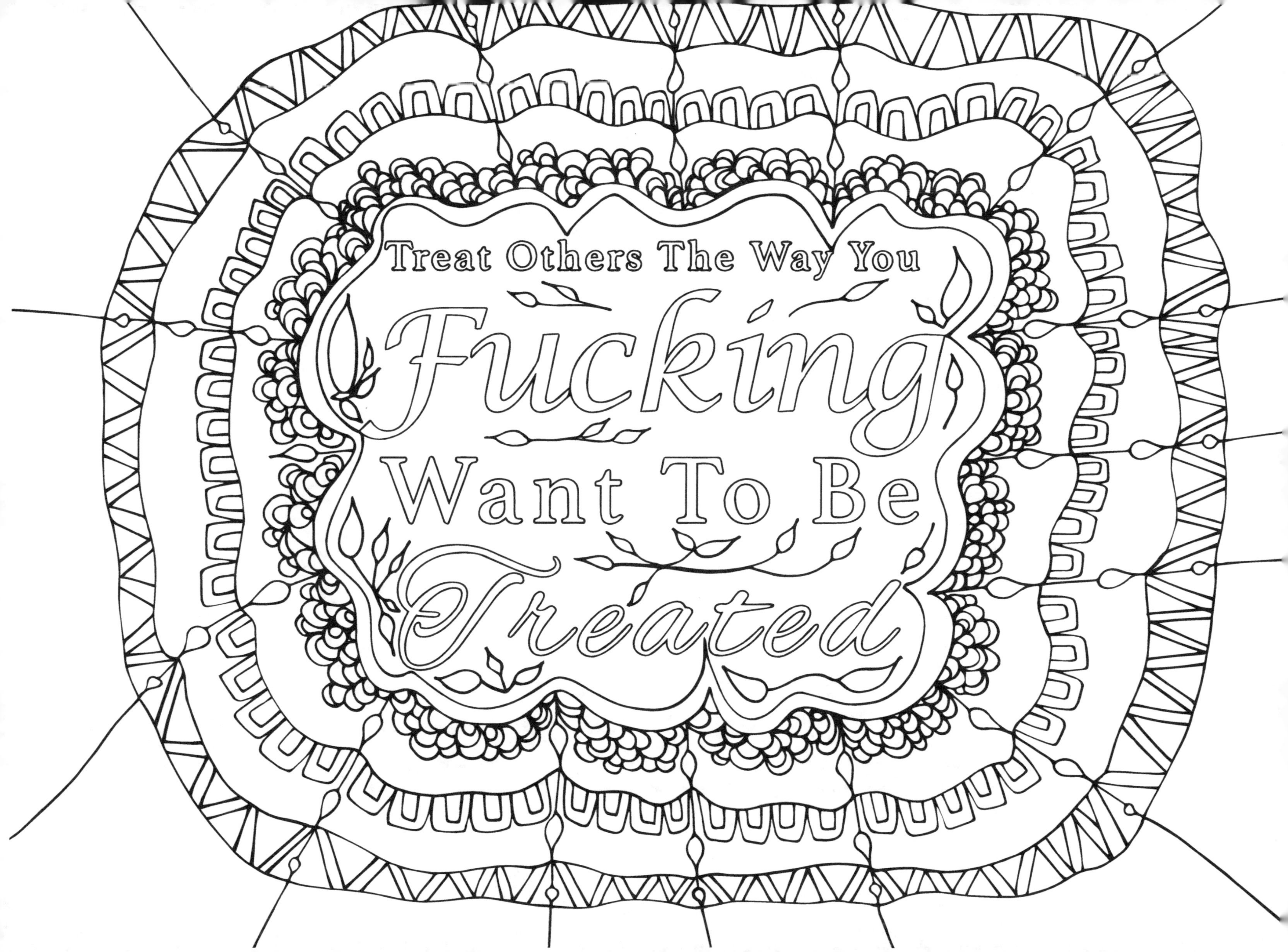

Treat Others The Way You
Fucking
Want To Be
Treated

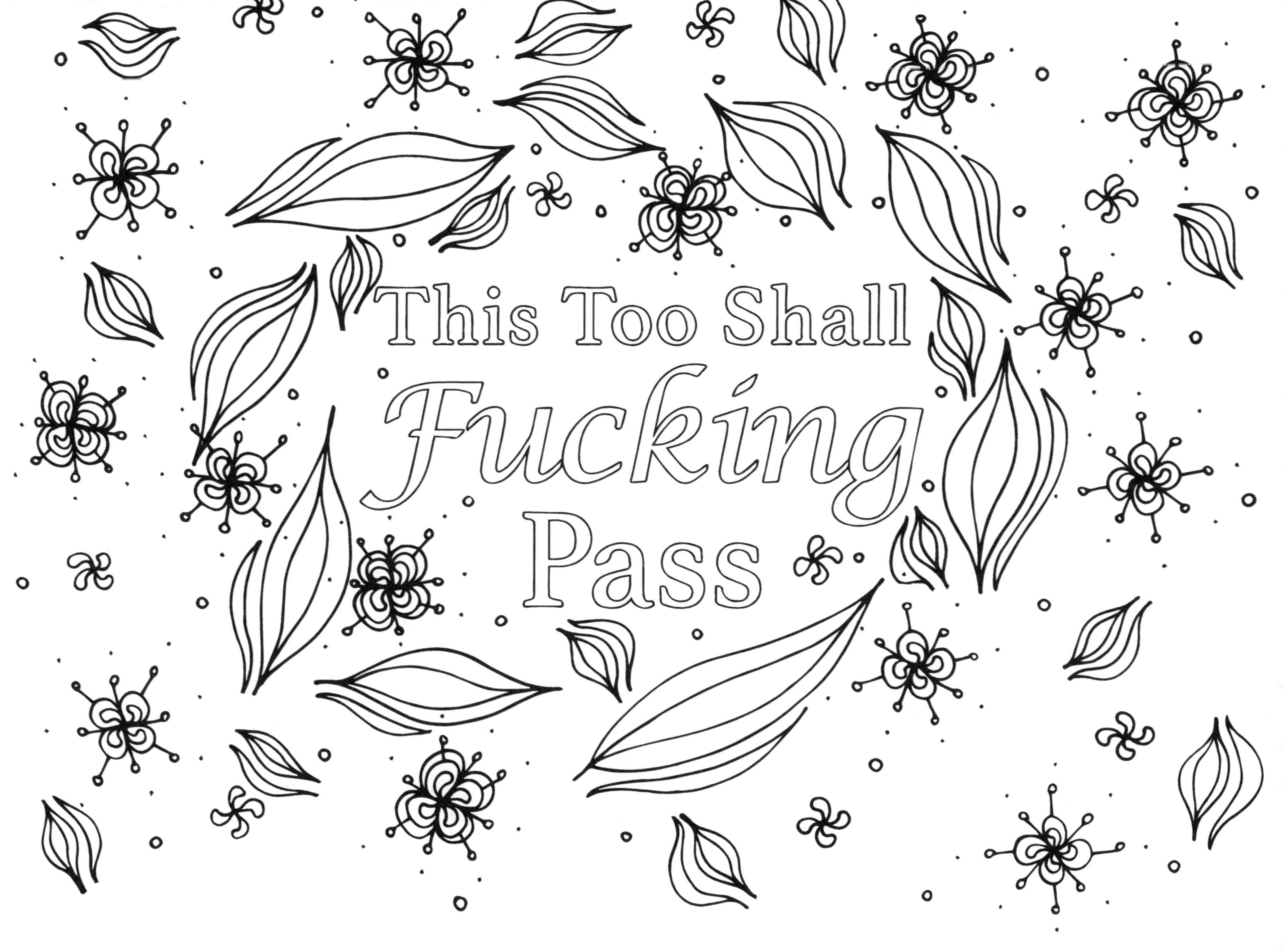
This Too Shall
Fucking
Pass

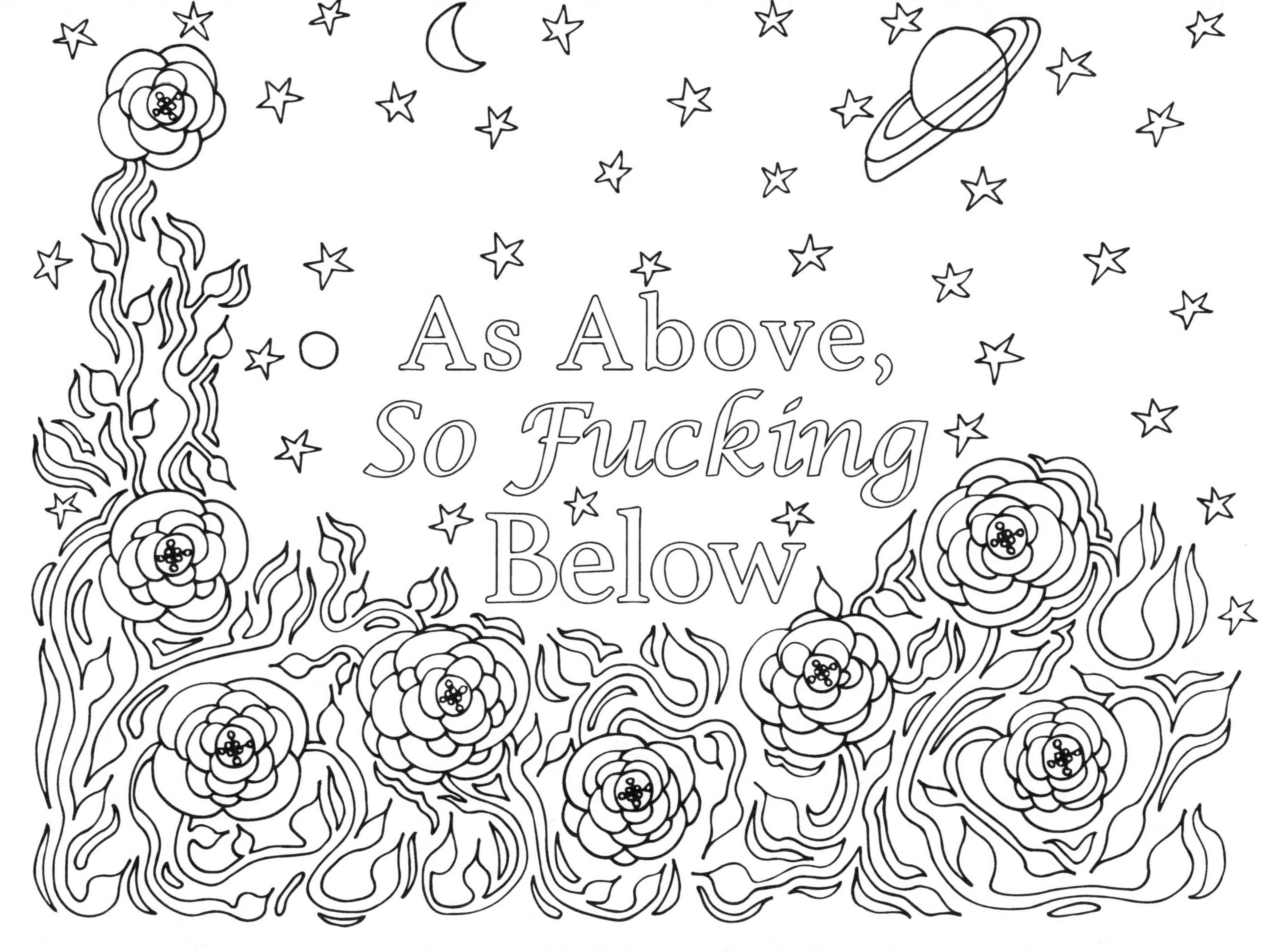

As Above,
So Fucking
Below

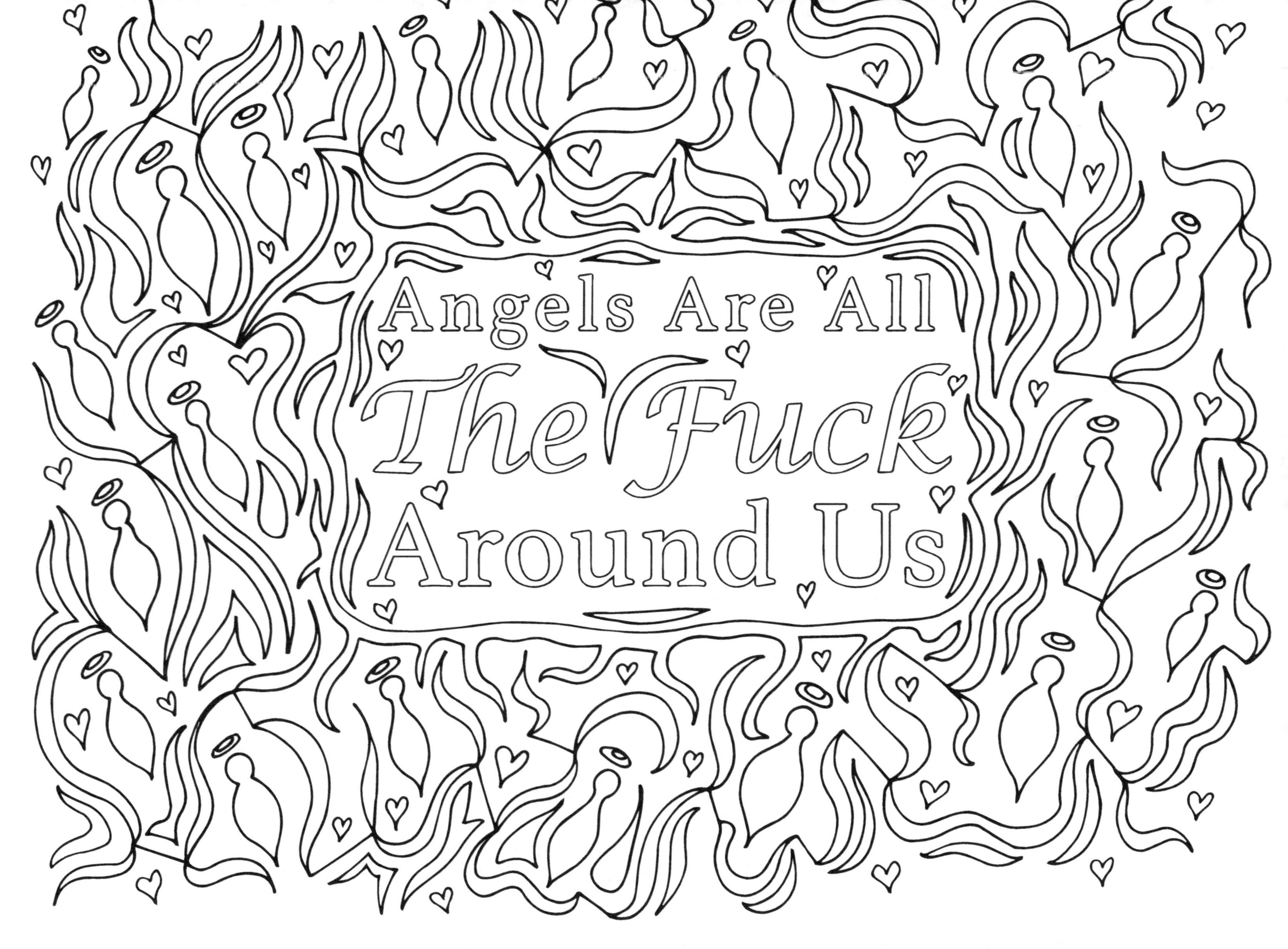

Angels Are All
The Fuck
Around Us

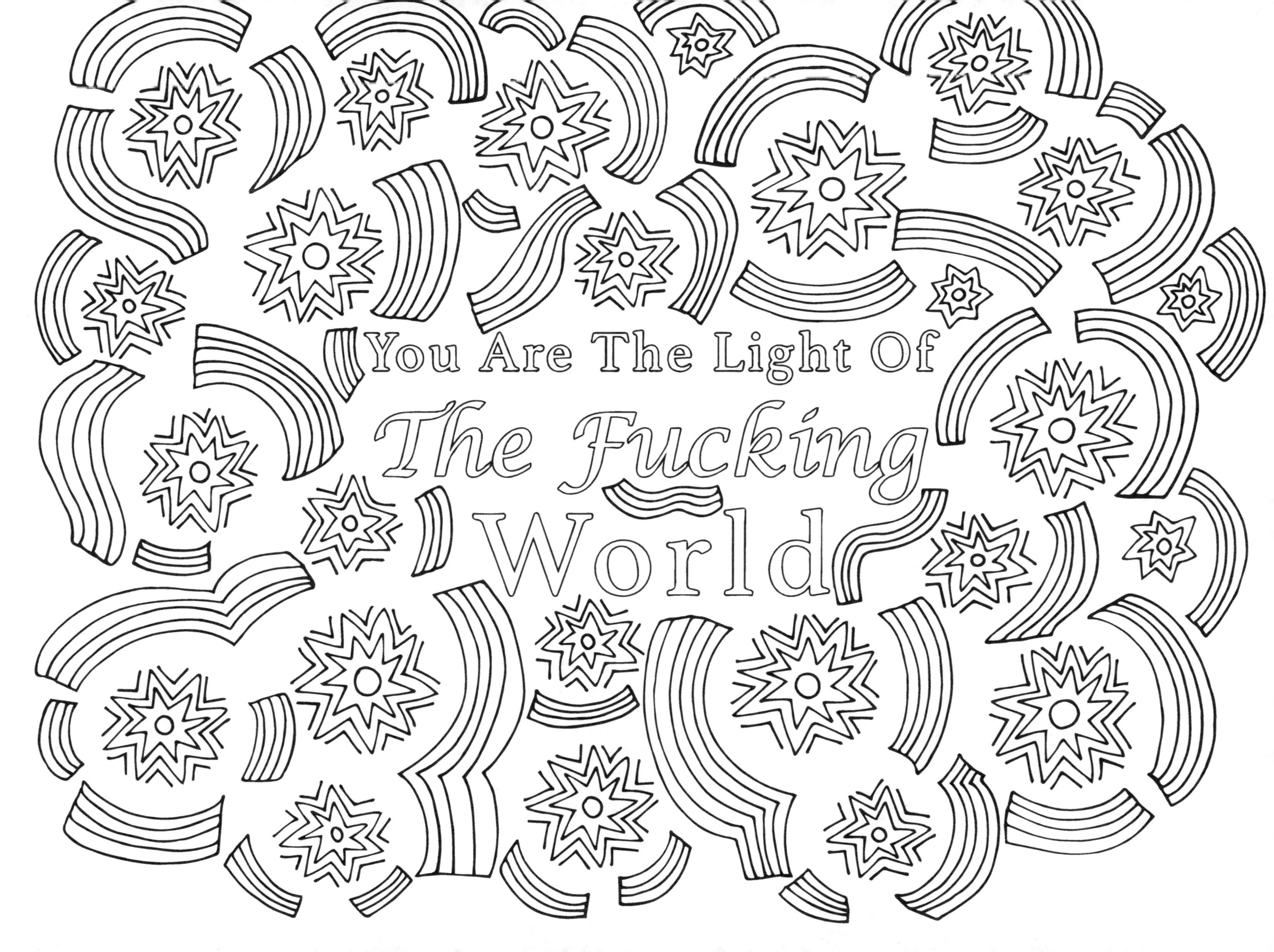

You Are The Light Of
The Fucking
World

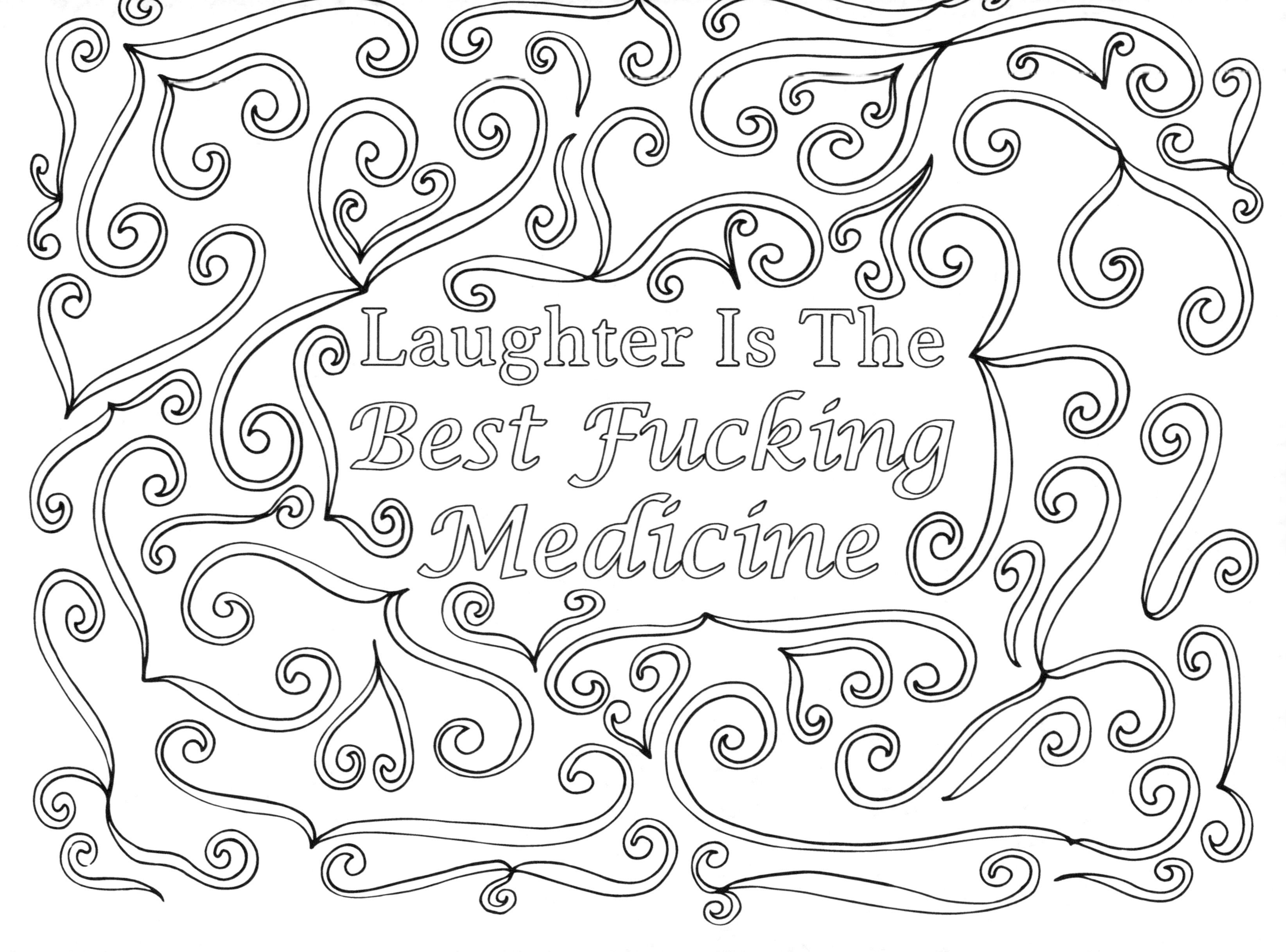

Laughter Is The
Best Fucking
Medicine

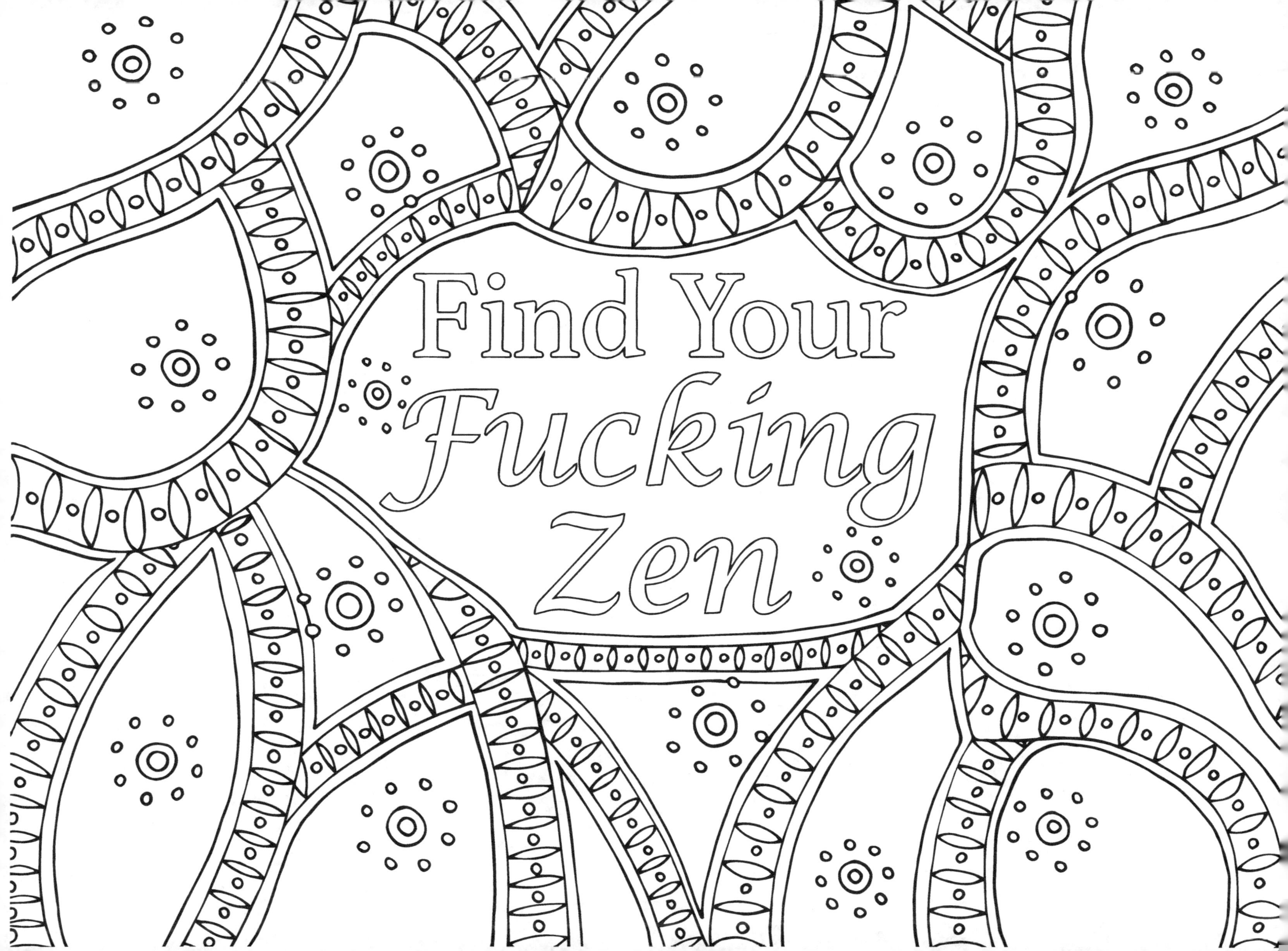

Find Your
Fucking
Zen

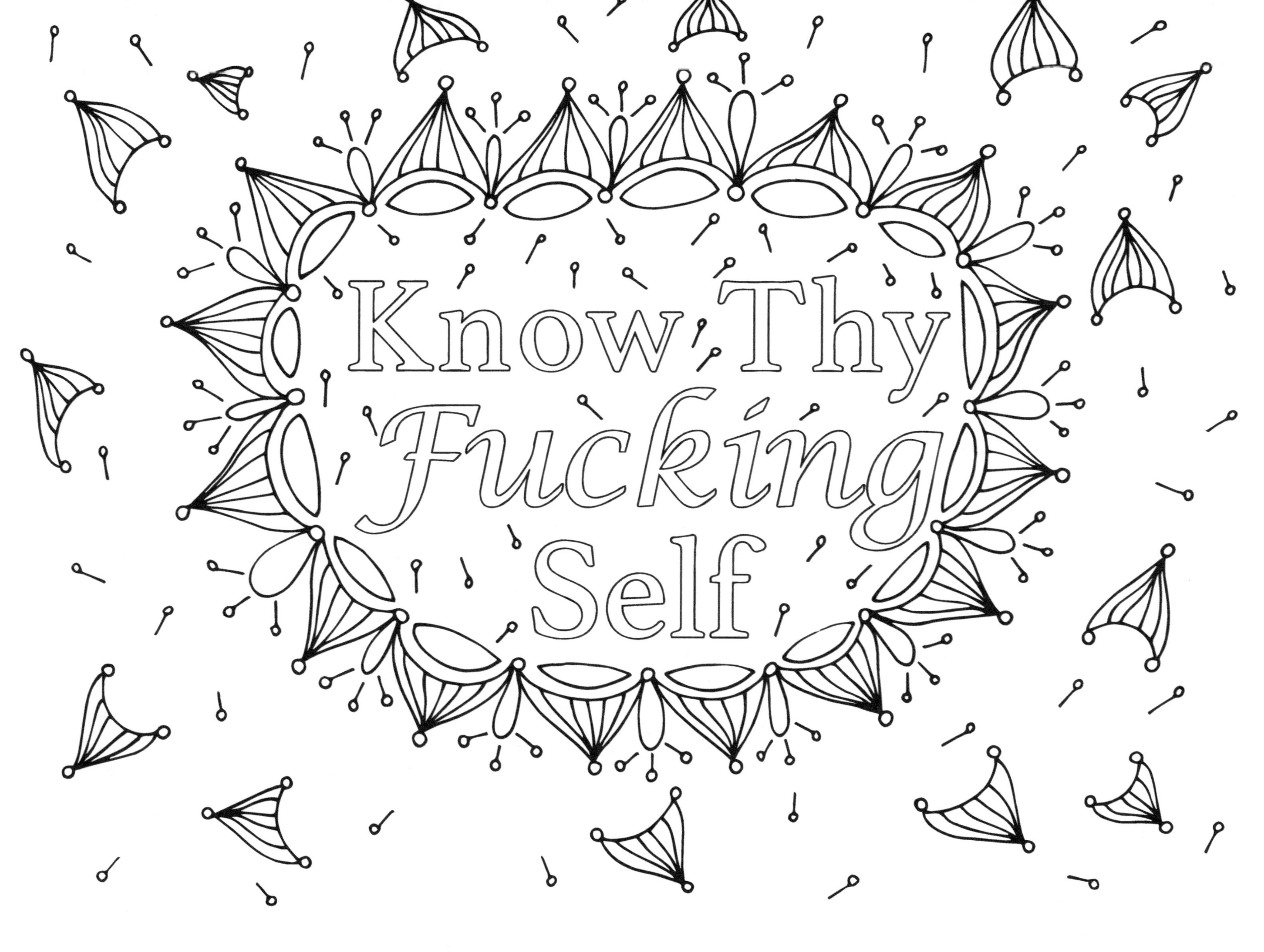

Know Thy
Fucking
Self

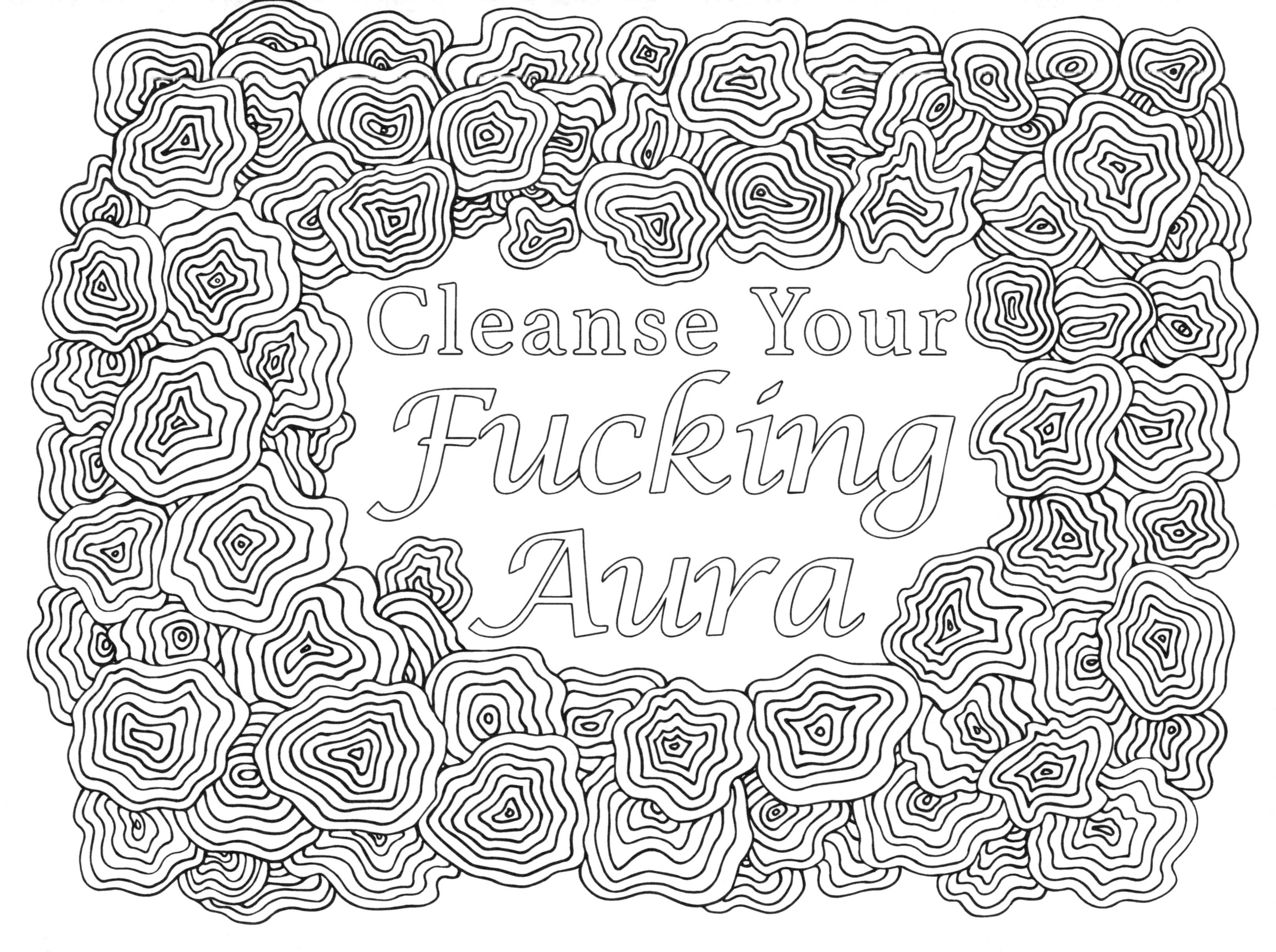

Cleanse Your
Fucking
Aura

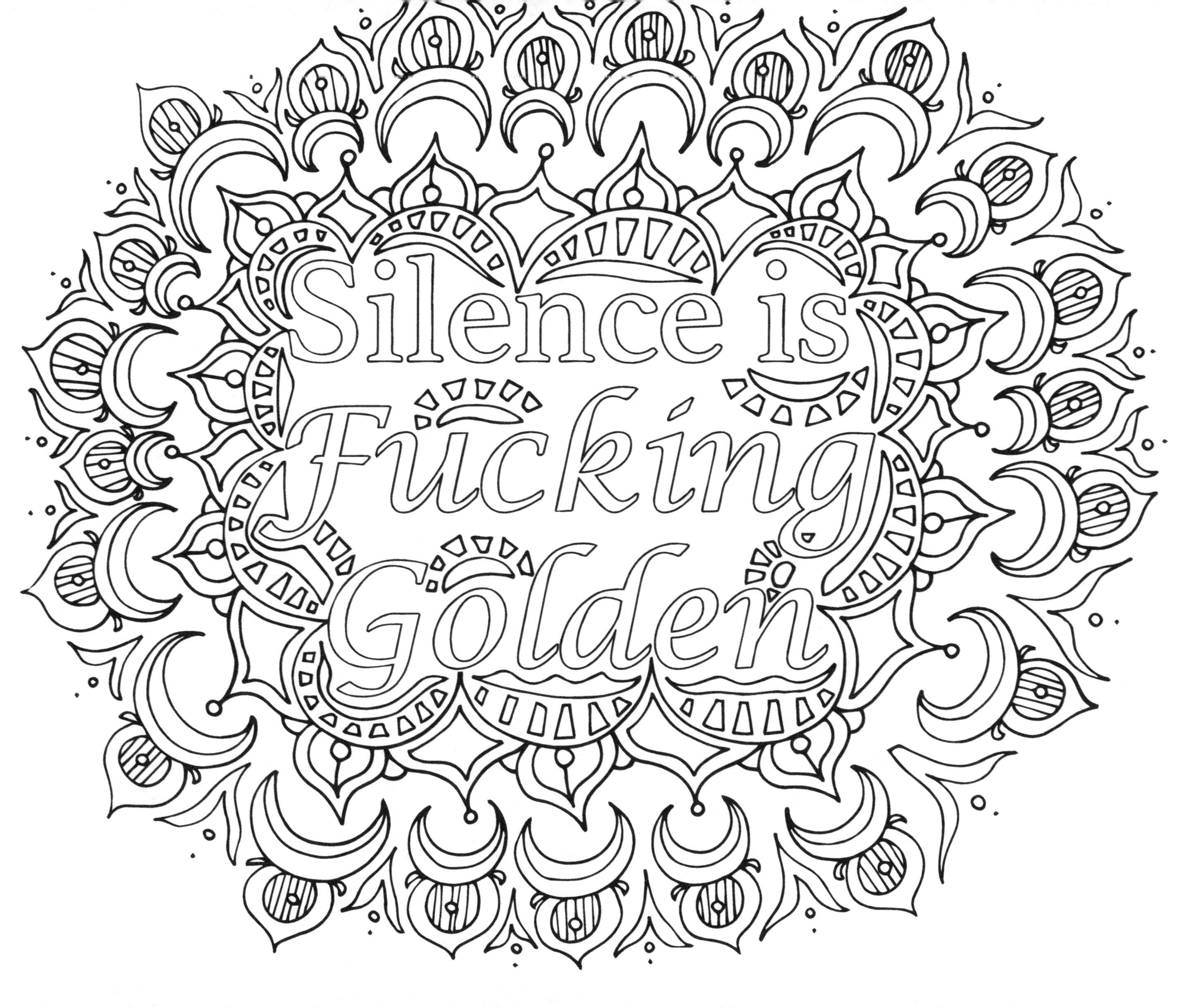

Silence is
Fucking
Golden

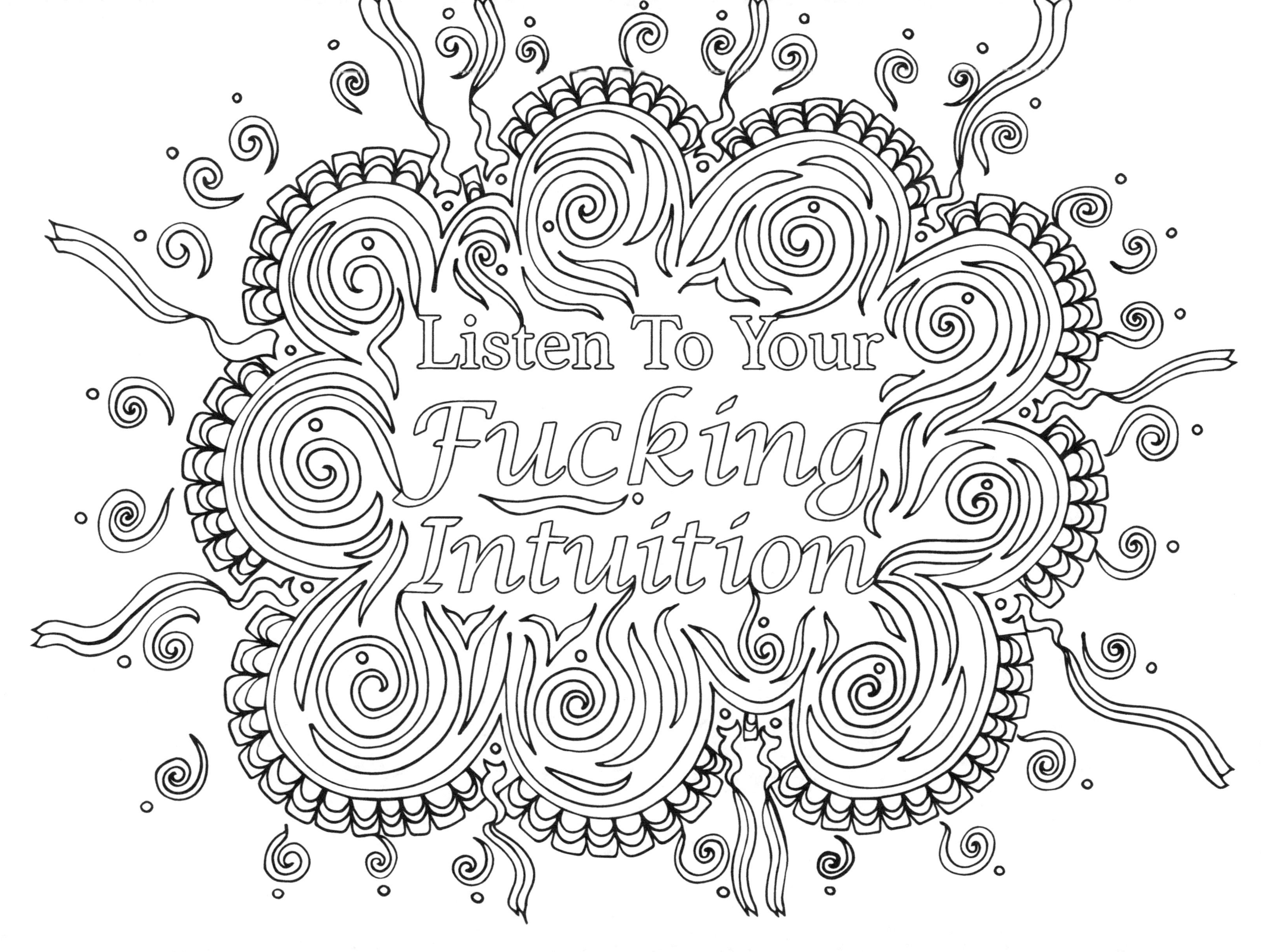

Listen To Your
Fucking
Intuition

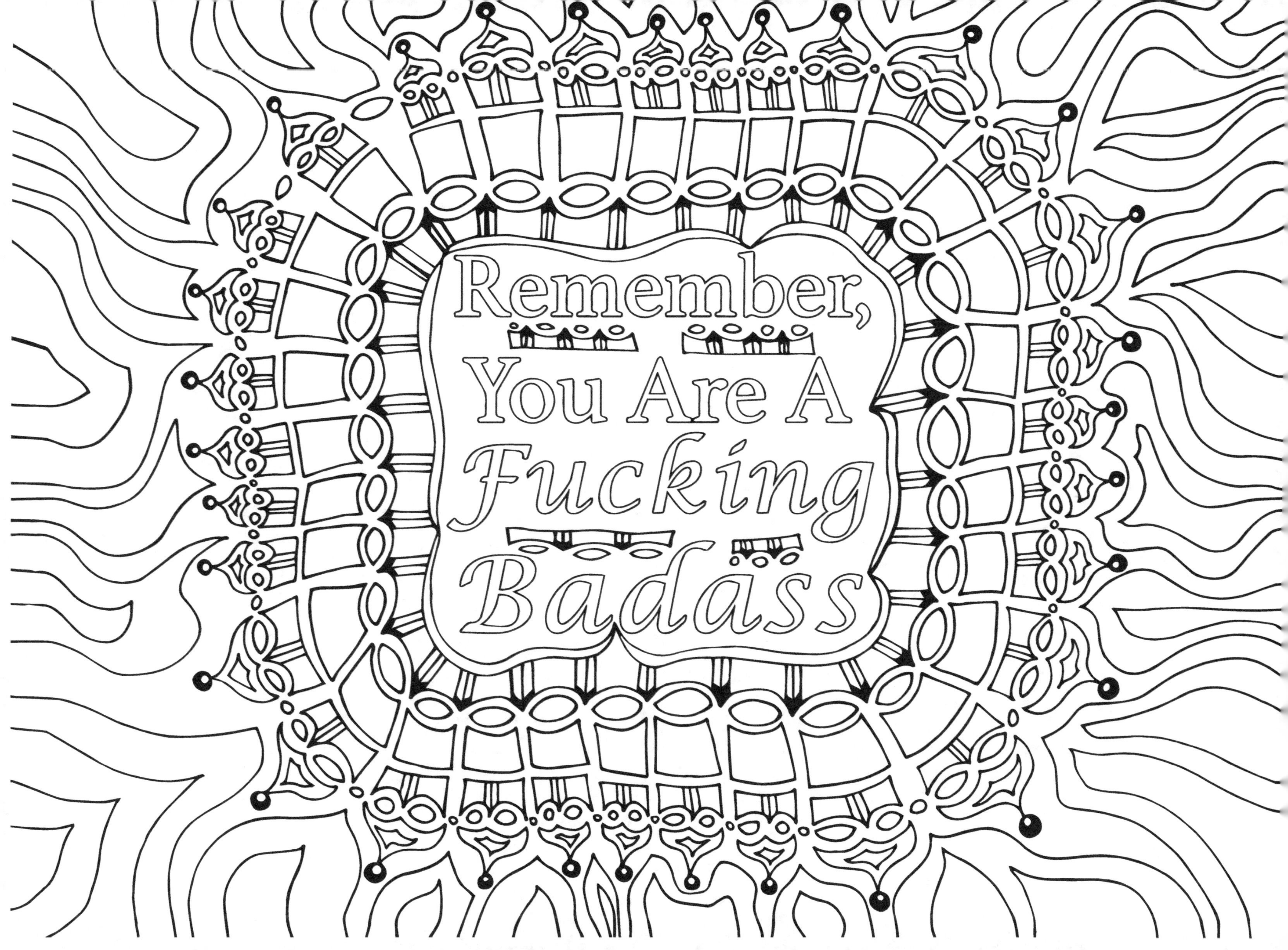

Remember,
You Are A
Fucking
Badass

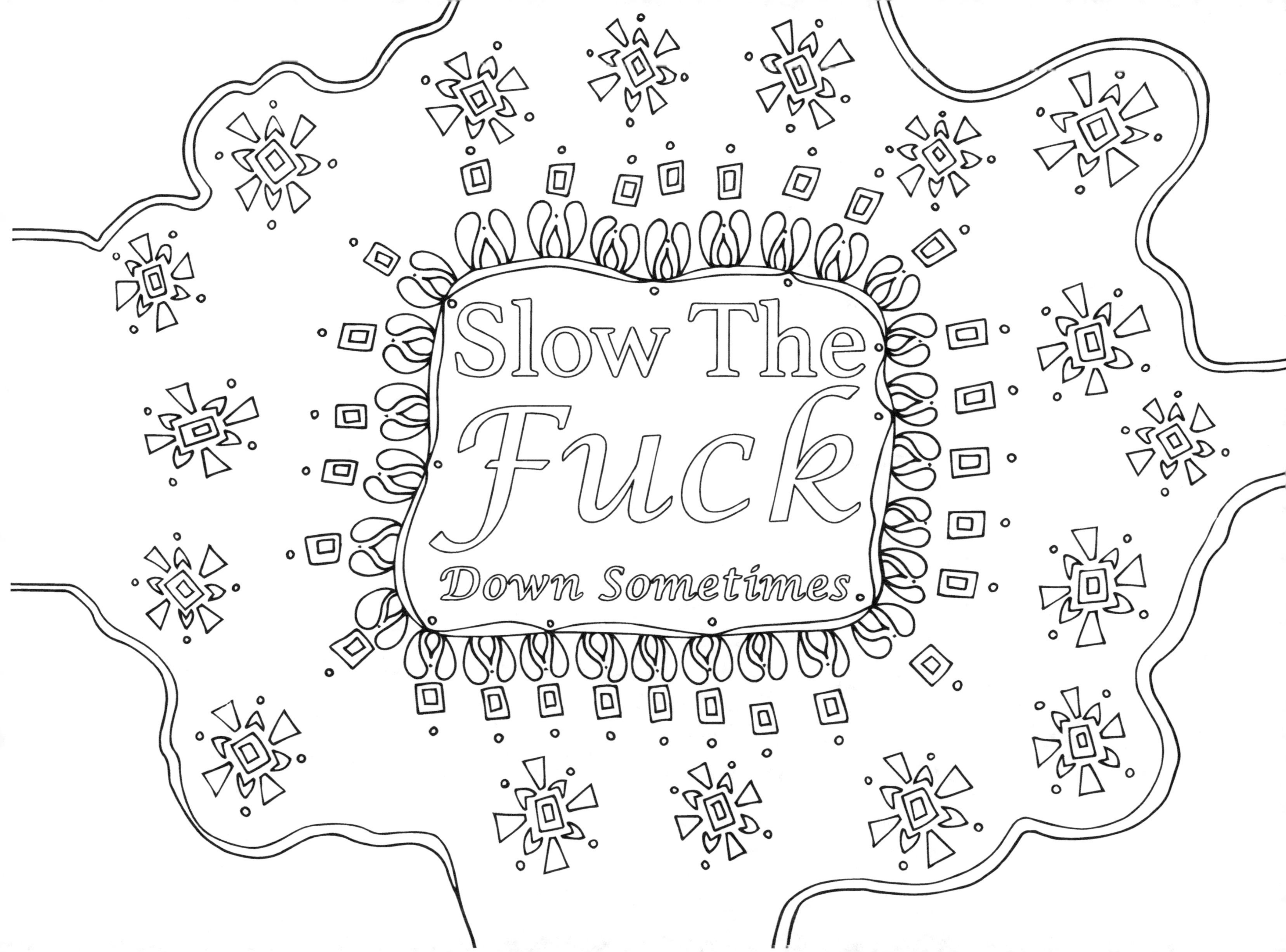

Slow The
Fuck
Down Sometimes

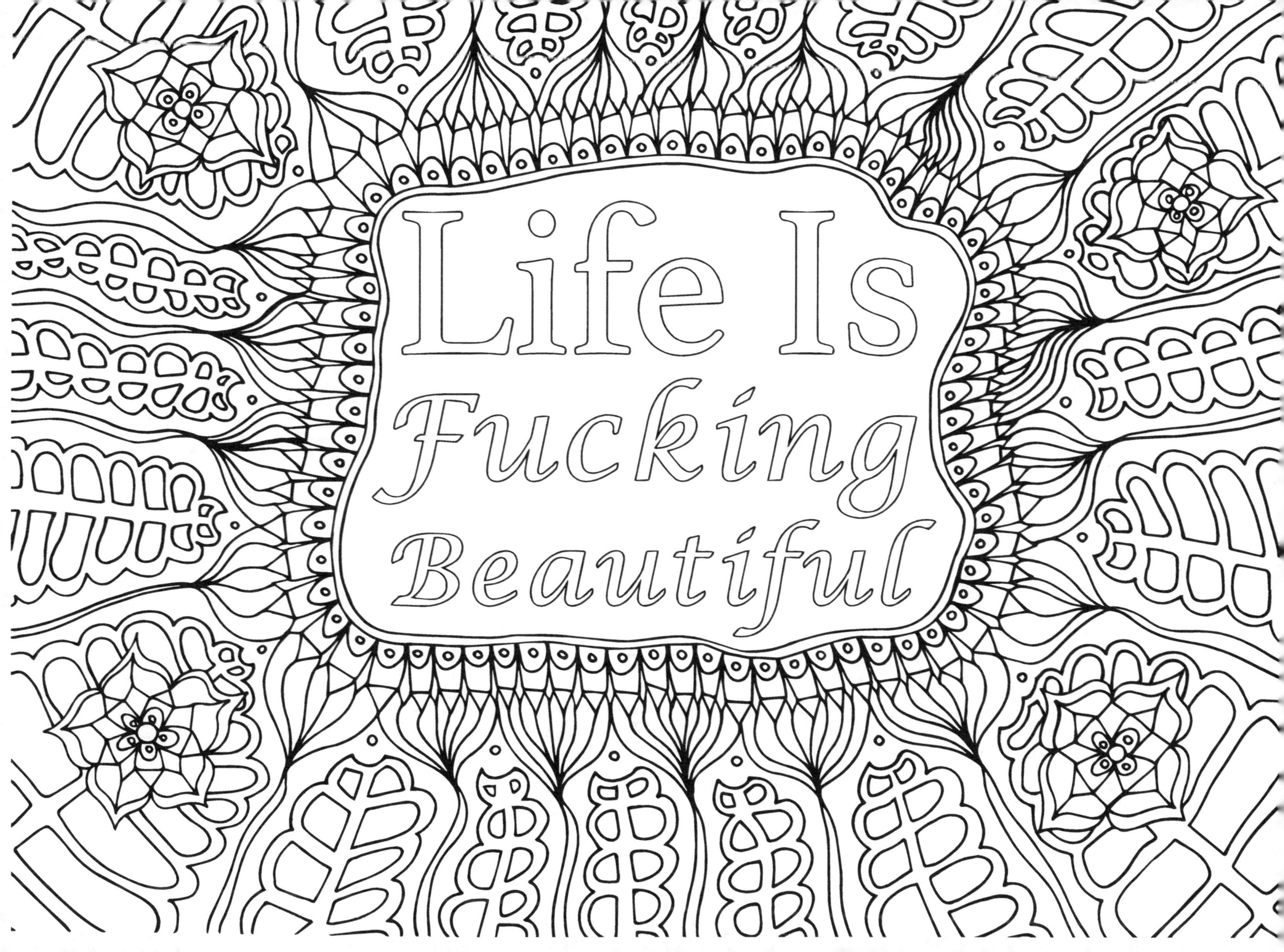

Life Is
Fucking
Beautiful